Power Maths

Year 4
Textbook 4A

GW00579082

Sparks
Sparks is helpful.
He likes to help if you get stuck.

flexible

Flo

brave

Astrid

curious

Ash

determined

Dexter

Series editor: Tony Staneff
Lead author: Josh Lury
Consultants (first edition): Professor Liu Jian and Professor Zhang Dan
Author team (first edition) Tony Staneff, Josh Lury, Neil Jarrett, Stephen Monaghan, Beth Smith and Paul Wrangles

Contents

This tells you which page you need.

Let's begin!

How to use this book

These pages make sure we're ready for the unit ahead. Find out what we'll be learning and brush up on your skills.

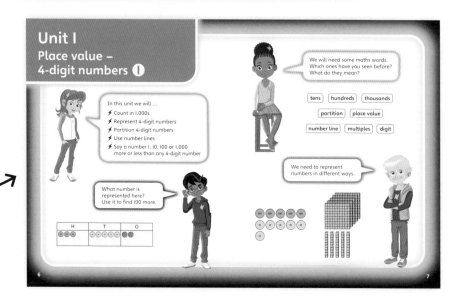

Discover

Lessons start with **Discover**.

Here, we explore new maths problems.

Can you work out how to find the answer?

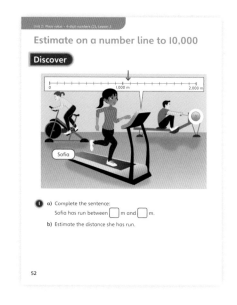

Don't be afraid to make mistakes. Learn from them and try again!

Share

Next, we share our ideas with the class.

Did we all solve the problems the same way? What ideas can you try?

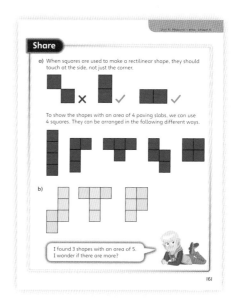

Think together

Then we have a go at some more problems together. Use what you have just learnt to help you.

We'll try a challenge too!

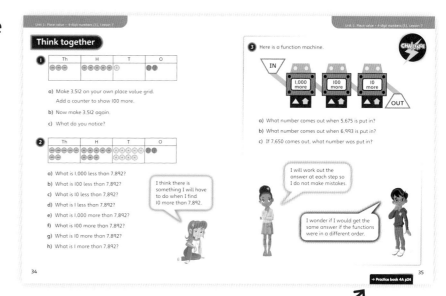

This tells you which page to go to in your **Practice Book**.

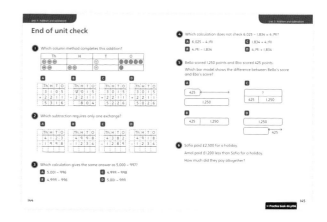

At the end of each unit there's an **End of unit check**. This is our chance to show how much we have learnt.

Unit 1
Place value – 4-digit numbers ❶

In this unit we will …

⚡ Count in 1,000s

⚡ Represent 4-digit numbers

⚡ Partition 4-digit numbers

⚡ Use number lines

⚡ Say a number 1, 10, 100 or 1,000 more or less than any 4-digit number

What number is represented here? Use it to find 100 more.

H	T	O
100 100 100	10 10 10 10 10	1 1

We will need some maths words. Which ones have you seen before? What do they mean?

tens   hundreds   thousands

partition   place value

number line   multiples   digit

We need to represent numbers in different ways.

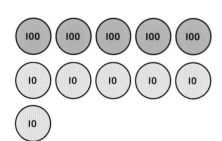

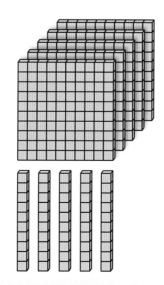

Represent and partition numbers to 1,000

Discover

There are 365 days in one year.

But what about leap years? There is one more day in a leap year.

1 **a)** Make 365 from base 10 equipment.

b) Show how 366 can be partitioned.

Share

a)

H	T	O
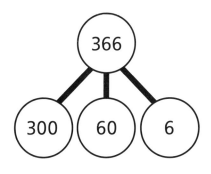		
3	6	5

The number has 3 digits: some 100s, some 10s and some 1s.

b) The number 366 has:
3 hundreds, 6 tens and 6 ones.

366
300 60 6

100 100 100 3×100

10 10 10 10 10 10 6×10

1 1 1 1 1 1 6×1

300 + 60 + 6 = 366

I wrote an addition to show the partitions.

Think together

1 Make 234 using base 10 equipment.

What is the value of each digit?

I will use a place value grid to help me.

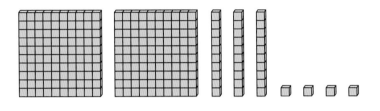

2 a) Complete the part-whole models.

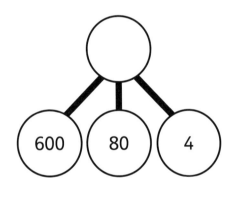

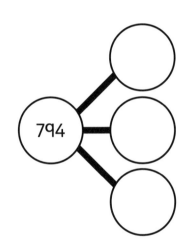

b) Complete these additions.

$\boxed{}$ = 600 + 80 + 4

794 = $\boxed{}$ + $\boxed{}$ + $\boxed{}$

c) What do you notice about your part-wholes and additions?

3 **a)** What number does each drawing represent?

A
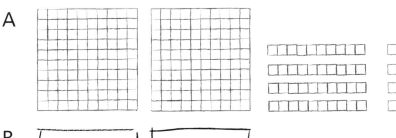

B

C

D
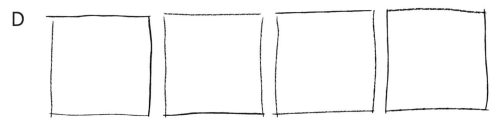

b) Which of these numbers has 0 tens?

I wonder if there's an easy way to see which of these has no 10s.

c) Draw base 10 equipment to represent these numbers:
305, 350, 353, 503.

11

→ Practice book 4A p6

Number line to 1,000

Discover

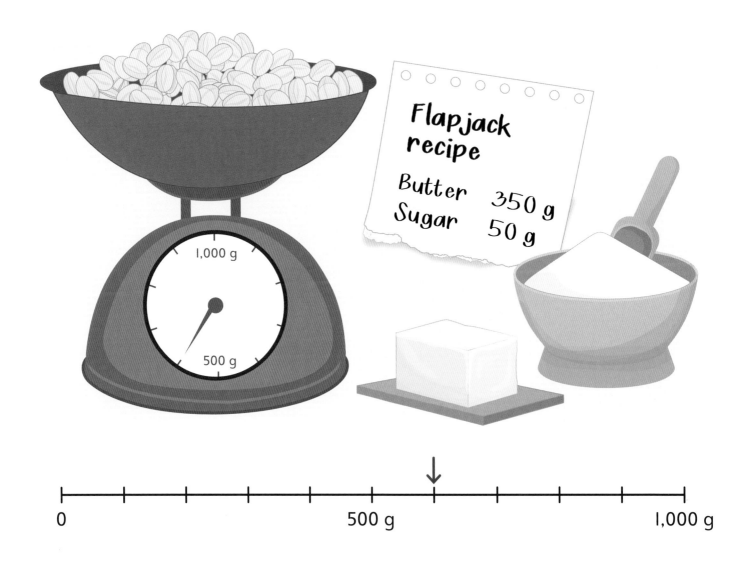

1 **a)** How many grams of oats are on the scales?

b) Where would the arrows for butter and sugar be on the scales?

Share

a) There are 600 g of oats on the scales.
The number line has intervals for each 100 g.

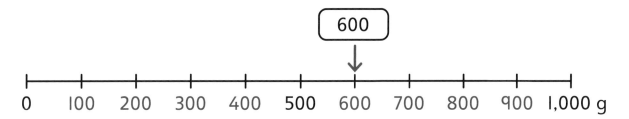

b) The arrow would point to 350 g of butter on
the scales. 350 is half-way between 300 and 400.

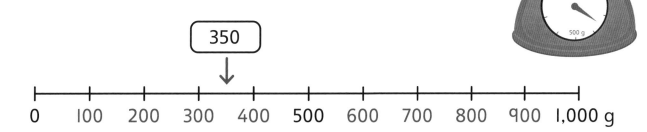

The arrow would point to 50 g of sugar on
the scales. 50 is half-way between 0 and 100.

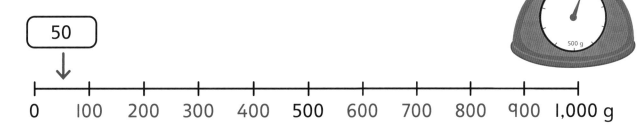

Think together

1 Count forwards and backwards on each number line.

What numbers do the arrows point to?

a)

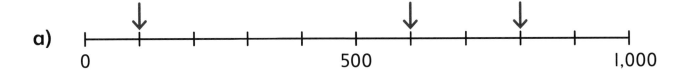

b)

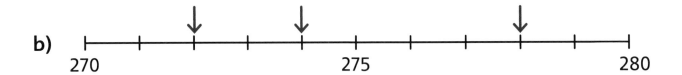

2 Count forwards and backwards on each number line.

Place 449 on each number line.

a)

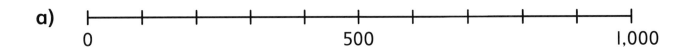

b)

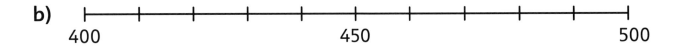

c)

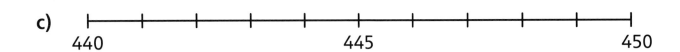

3 **a)** Estimate how much water is in the jug.

b) Estimate the length of the stick.

c) Estimate the heights of the bars.

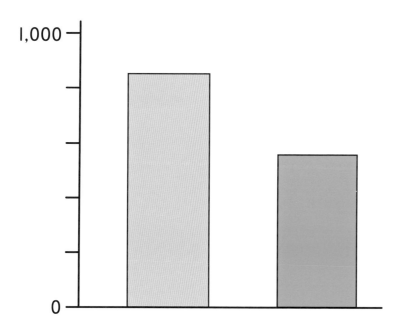

15

Multiples of 1,000

Discover

1 **a)** Count the lemon sweets on the forklift pallet.

   Count the strawberry sweets on the forklift pallet.

   b) How many sweets are there altogether?

Share

a) Count the multiples of 1,000.

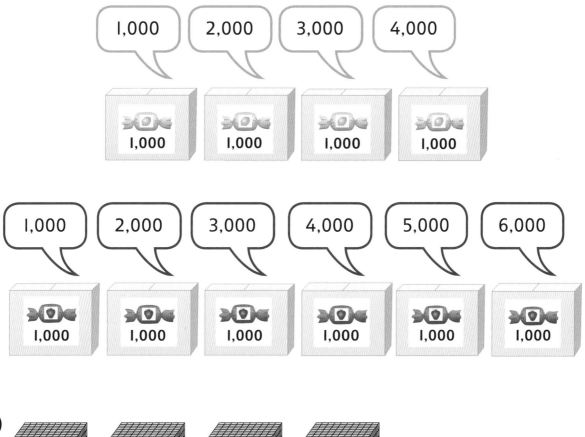

b)

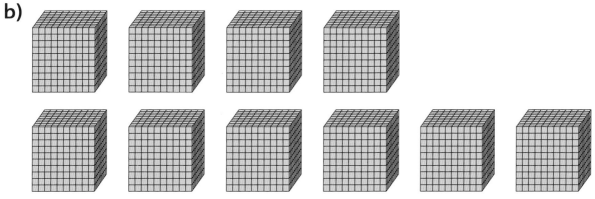

$$4 \quad + \quad 6 \quad = \quad 10$$

$$4 \text{ thousand} \quad + \quad 6 \text{ thousand} \quad = \quad 10 \text{ thousand}$$

$$4,000 \quad + \quad 6,000 \quad = \quad 10,000$$

Think together

 a) Count the strawberry sweets.

b) Count the lemon sweets.

c) How many sweets altogether?

2 Complete the number tracks.

a)

0	1,000	2,000			5,000		7,000

b)

	2,000		4,000	

c)

6,000		8,000		

d)

8,000		6,000			3,000

③

CHALLENGE

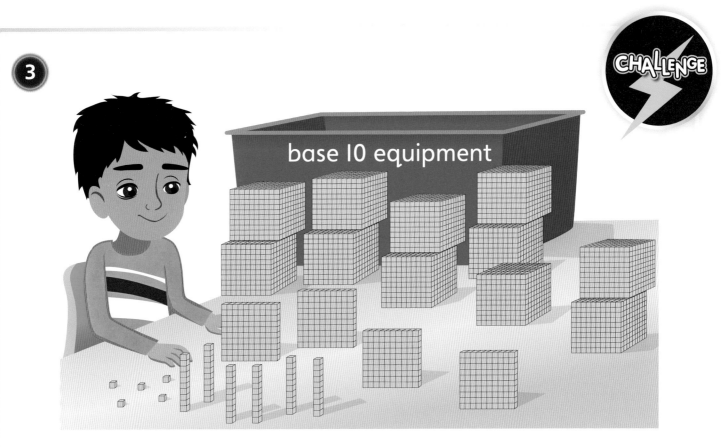

base 10 equipment

Why does a big cube, or block, of base 10 equipment mean 1 thousand?

a) How could you make 1,000 using 100s?

b) How could you make 1,000 using 10s?

c) How could you make 1,000 using 1s?

d) How could you make 2,000 using 100s?

e) How could you make 2,000 using 10s?

f) How could you make 2,000 using 1s?

19

→ Practice book 4A p12

4-digit numbers

Discover

1 **a)** Choose three of the cards.

Make a 3-digit number.

Make your number from base 10 equipment.

b) Place the remaining card at the front of the cards chosen to make a 4-digit number.

Make your number from base 10 equipment.

Share

a)

H	T	O
1	4	5

I could have made lots of different numbers.

b)

Th	H	T	O
2	1	4	5

I showed the numbers on a place value grid.

Think together

1   Say and write the numbers shown.

Th	H	T	O
1,000 1,000 1,000	100 100 100 100	10 10 10 10 10 10	1 1

Th	H	T	O
1,000 1,000 1,000 1,000	100 100	10 10 10 10 10	1 1 1 1 1 1

2   Say each number.

Make each number using place value counters.

3	2	5	0

3	2	0	5

3	0	2	5

A place value grid helps me.

22

3 Explore 4-digit numbers.

Use each card once to make a 4-digit number.

Make your number from place value counters.

Say the number out loud.

Write the number.

CHALLENGE

2	1
0	2

I will play with a partner. We can take it in turns and try to make different numbers each time.

I wonder if we can find all the possible 4-digit numbers.

23

Partition 4-digit numbers

Discover

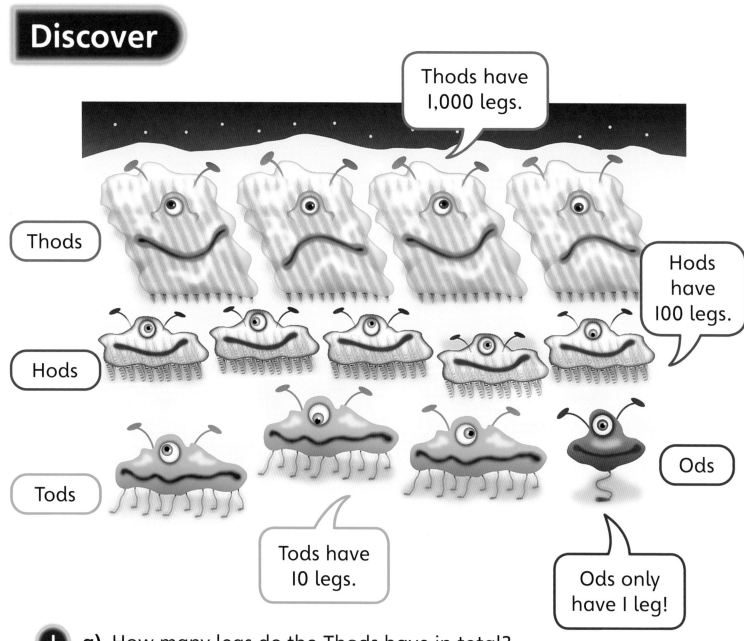

1 a) How many legs do the Thods have in total?

How many legs do the Hods have in total?

How many legs do the Tods have in total?

How many legs do the Ods have in total?

b) How many legs are there altogether?

Share

a)

| 4,000 | 500 | 30 | 1 |

I used place value counters to represent the legs.

b)

4,000   +   500   +   30   +   1   =   4,531

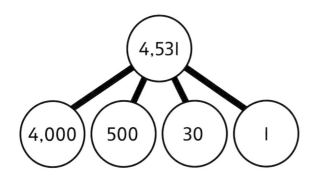

There are 4,531 legs altogether.

Think together

1 Partition 2,542 into 1,000s, 100s, 10s and 1s.

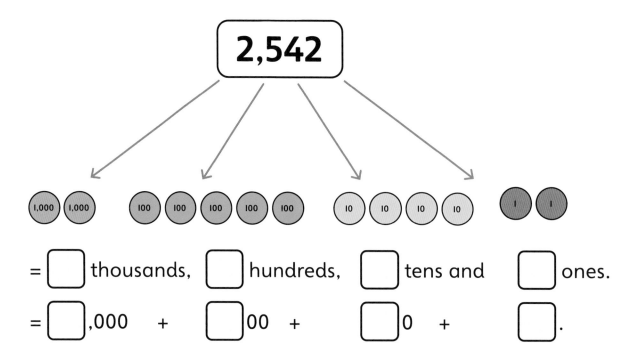

= ⬚ thousands, ⬚ hundreds, ⬚ tens and ⬚ ones.

= ⬚,000 + ⬚00 + ⬚0 + ⬚.

2 Complete each partitioning.

a)

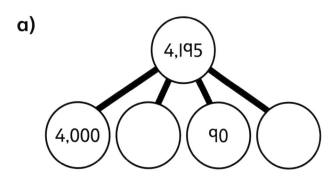

b) ⬚ = 3,000 + 200 + 70 + 5

c) ⬚ = 1 + 50 + 600 + 2,000

d) 5,219 = 5,000 + ⬚ + 10 + 9

3 **a)** What is the value of each digit?

5210   5201   5070

I will write each number on a place value grid.

Th	H	T	O

b) Complete each addition.

☐ = 3,000 + 30 + 3

☐ = 3 + 300 + 3,000

☐ = 9,000 + 9

☐ = 90 + 9,000

7,070 = ☐ + ☐ + ☐ + ☐

7,707 = ☐ + ☐ + ☐ + ☐

I thought all 4-digit numbers had to be partitioned into four parts. Maybe I am wrong.

27

→ Practice book 4A p18

Partition 4-digit numbers flexibly

Discover

1 a) Divide the parcels and letter between the three sacks.

b) What is the total mass of all the parcels and letter?

28

Share

a) Here are two ways you can divide the parcels and letter.

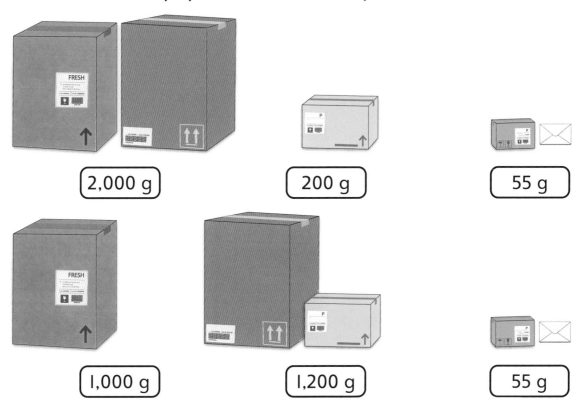

2,000 g   200 g   55 g

1,000 g   1,200 g   55 g

b) The total mass is the same, however you sort them.

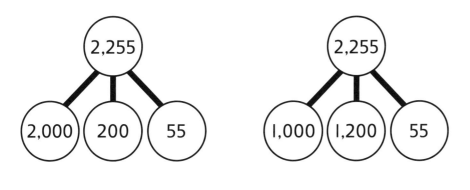

There are lots of ways I could have put the parcels and letter into the sacks.

Think together

1 Find five different ways to partition 3,225.

$$3,225 = 3,000 + 200 + 20 + 5$$

I will try to find a way no one else in my class has found.

I will partition into two parts, then three parts, then...

2 Complete the partitions.

a) $\boxed{} = 1,000 + 400 + 35$

b) $\boxed{} = 2,000 + 570 + 5$

c) $\boxed{} = 1,000 + 1,200 + 30 + 6$

d) $2,985 = 2,000 + 900 + \boxed{}$

e) $3,644 = 3,000 + 630 + \boxed{}$

f) $7,555 = 5,000 + \boxed{} + 50 + 5$

3 Use the part-whole models to solve the calculations.

a)

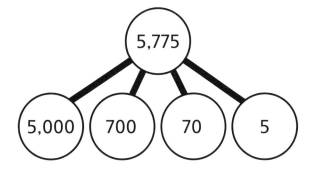

5,775 – 700 = ☐   5,775 – ☐ = 5,770

5,775 – 70 = ☐   5,775 – ☐ = 775

b)

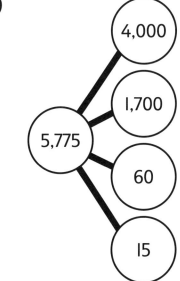

5,775 – 15 = ☐

5,775 – 60 = ☐

5,775 – ☐ = 4,065

5,775 – ☐ = 1,715

31

→ **Practice book 4A p21**

1, 10, 100, 1,000 more or less

Discover

Last week's attendance:
8,980

1 **a)** Make this number from place value counters on a place value grid.

b) This week, 1,000 more people attend.

Add a counter to the place value grid to show 1,000 more than 8,980.

Share

a)

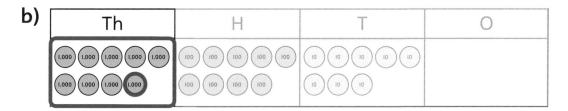

8 thousands   9 hundreds   8 tens   0 ones

b)

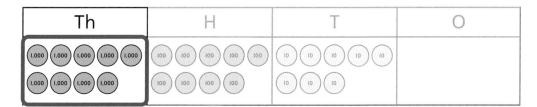

One more than 8 is 9.

One thousand more than 8 thousand is 9 thousand.

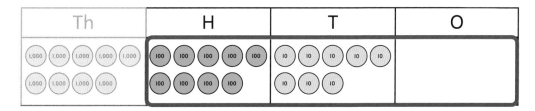

The thousand place increases to 9 thousand.

Th	H	T	O

9 thousands   9 hundreds   8 tens   0 ones

The other digits do **not change**.

1,000 more than 8,980 is 9,980.

Think together

Th	H	T	O
1,000 1,000 1,000	100 100 100 100 100 10		• •

a) Make 3,512 on your own place value grid.

Add a counter to show 100 more.

b) Now make 3,512 again.

c) What do you notice?

2

Th	H	T	O
1,000 1,000 1,000 1,000 1,000 1,000 1,000	100 100 100 100 100 100 100 100	10 10 10 10 10 10 10 10 10	• •

a) What is 1,000 less than 7,892?

b) What is 100 less than 7,892?

c) What is 10 less than 7,892?

d) What is 1 less than 7,892?

e) What is 1,000 more than 7,892?

f) What is 100 more than 7,892?

g) What is 10 more than 7,892?

h) What is 1 more than 7,892?

> I think there is something I will have to do when I find 10 more than 7,892.

3 Here is a function machine.

a) What number comes out when 5,675 is put in?

b) What number comes out when 6,993 is put in?

c) If 7,650 comes out, what number was put in?

I will work out the answer at each step so I do not make mistakes.

I wonder if I would get the same answer if the functions were in a different order.

→ **Practice book 4A p24**

1,000s, 100s, 10s and 1s

Discover

Next up, the fifteen hundred metres race.

1 **a)** Use base 10 equipment to show 'fifteen hundred' in 100s.

b) Use base 10 equipment to show 'fifteen hundred' in 1,000s and 100s.

Share

a)

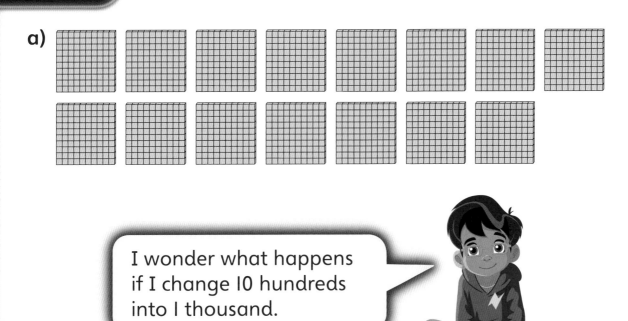

I wonder what happens if I change 10 hundreds into 1 thousand.

b) 10 hundreds is equal to 1 thousand.

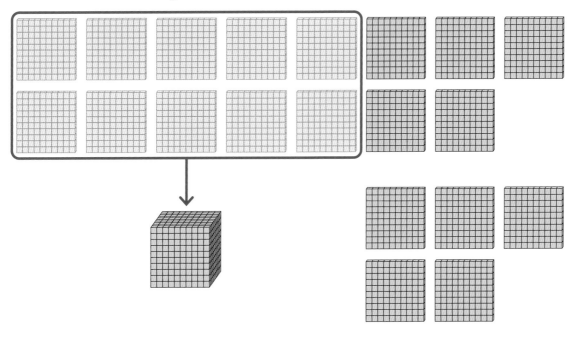

'Fifteen hundred' is 1 thousand and 5 hundreds.

Think together

1 a) Write each number as a 4-digit number.

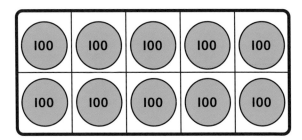 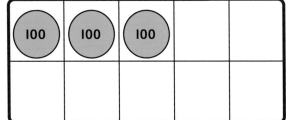

13 hundreds is equal to ☐.

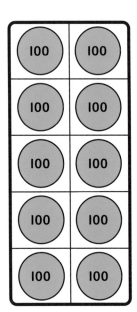 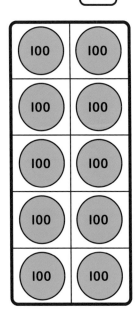 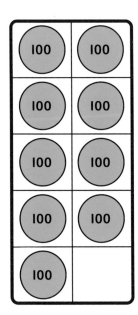

☐ hundreds is equal to ☐.

2 Make these numbers from place value counters.

Write them as 4-digit numbers.

I cycled 25 hundred miles in August.

14 hundred visitors came to the zoo today.

3 How many 100 g weights will make 2,500 g?

How many 10 g weights will make 2,500 g?

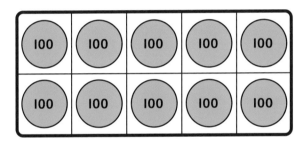

I will think about 10 hundreds.

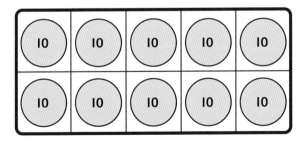

I wonder if thinking about 10 tens helps.

39

→ Practice book 4A p27

End of unit check

1 What number is represented here?

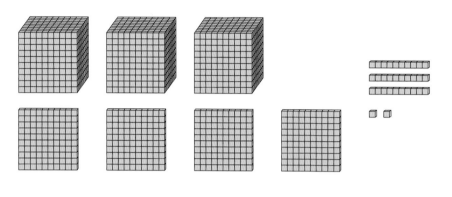

A 4,332   B 7,023   C 3,423   D 3,432

2 What number is represented here?

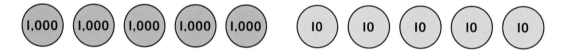

A 5,500   B 55   C 5,050   D 5,005

3 What number does the part-whole model show?

A Five hundred and sixty-eight

B Five thousand and sixty-eight

C 5,000,608

D 568

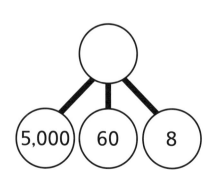

4 What number is the arrow pointing to?

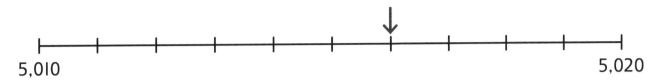

5,010   5,020

A 5,106   B 5,015   C 5,506   D 5,016

5 Complete the partition.

4,657 = 3,000 + ⬜ + 50 + 7

A 600   B 1,000   C 1,600   D 4,000

6 Use three of the digit cards to make the number shown on the number line.

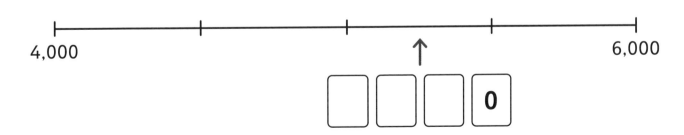

4,000   6,000

⬜⬜⬜ 0

41

→ Practice book 4A p30

Unit 2
Place value – 4-digit numbers ②

In this unit we will ...

⚡ Find missing numbers on number lines

⚡ Estimate numbers on number lines

⚡ Compare and order numbers to 10,000

⚡ Round numbers to the nearest 1,000, 100 and 10

Do you remember how to count in 100s?

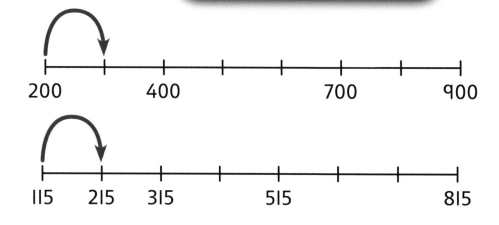

200   400   700   900

115   215   315   515   815

We will need some maths words. Which ones have we used before?

thousands   ascending   descending

round   order   multiple

round up   round down

greater than (>)   less than (<)

We will need this too! Use it to find the next multiple of 1,000.

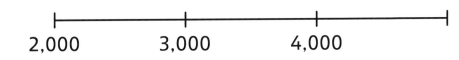

2,000   3,000   4,000

Number line to 10,000

Discover

1 **a)** Draw a number line from 0 to 10,000.

Label each multiple of 1,000.

Label where Emma places her number card.

b) Draw a number line from 1,000 to 2,000.

Label each multiple of 100.

Label where Luis places his number card.

Share

a) This number line goes from 0 to 10,000, with each multiple of 1,000 labelled.

0 is a multiple of 1,000.

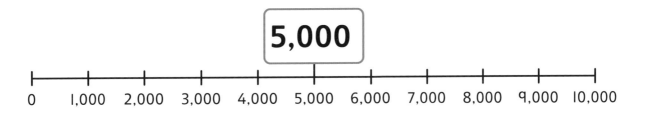

b) This is like zooming in on the number line with a magnifying glass.

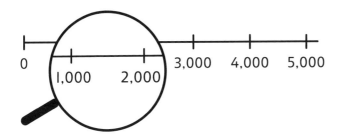

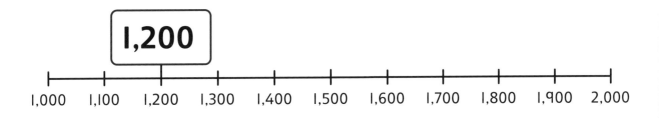

1,000 and 2,000 are also multiples of 100.

I mm is **tiny**. I wonder how long 10,000 mm is. I will measure it myself.

Think together

1 What are the missing multiples of 10?

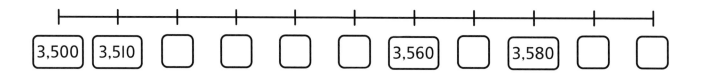

3,500 3,510 ☐ ☐ ☐ ☐ 3,560 ☐ 3,580 ☐ ☐

2 What numbers are the arrows pointing to?

a)

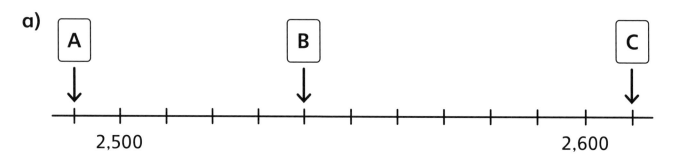

b)

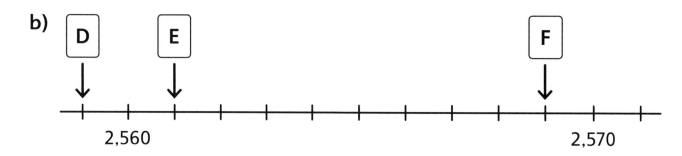

First, I will work out if the number lines go up in 1s, 10s or bigger jumps.

3 Max counts in 10s.

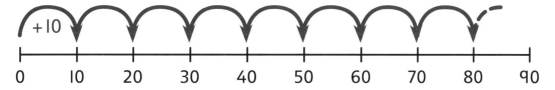

Reena counts in 100s.

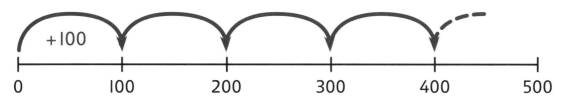

Danny counts in 1,000s.

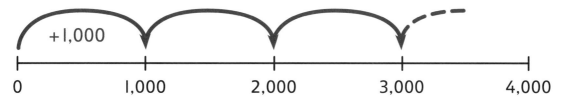

Which of these numbers will Danny say?

Which of these numbers will Reena say?

Which of these numbers will Max say?

4,500	2,100
2,000	2,010
3,290	3,900
10,000	5,000
9,990	9,999
1,200	1,010
1,235	6,005

Reena   Max   Danny

Which numbers will all three children say?

47

Between two multiples

Discover

1 a) Draw a number line from 0 to 10,000.

Label the multiples of 1,000.

Andy's number is between two multiples. Which ones?

b) Show the part of the line for Bella's number.

Share

a)

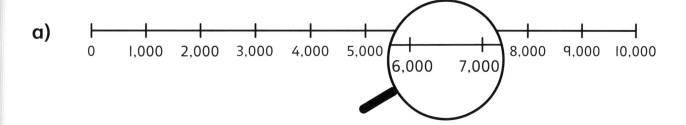

Previous thousand

6,000

6,790

Next thousand

7,000

Andy's number falls between 6,000 and 7,000.

b)

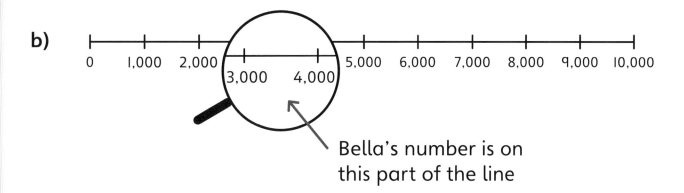

Bella's number is on this part of the line

Previous thousand

3,000

?

Next thousand

4,000

I wonder what number it is. Can I work out any of its digits?

Think together

1 Say a number that goes in the shaded part of each number line.

a)

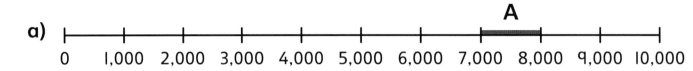

b)

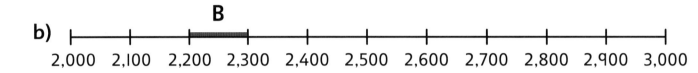

c)

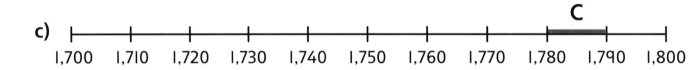

2

For each number:

a) What is the previous and next multiple of 100?

b) What is the previous and next multiple of 10?

I wonder if I can find a pattern. That might help me.

I need to use a different number line for each of these.

3 Write down the previous and next multiples.

CHALLENGE

a) Previous thousand   Next thousand

[ ]   4,999   [ ]

b) Previous hundred   Next hundred

[ ]   4,999   [ ]

c) Previous ten   Next ten

[ ]   4,999   [ ]

I noticed something strange. Let me explore this further.

→ Practice book 4A p35

Estimate on a number line to 10,000

Discover

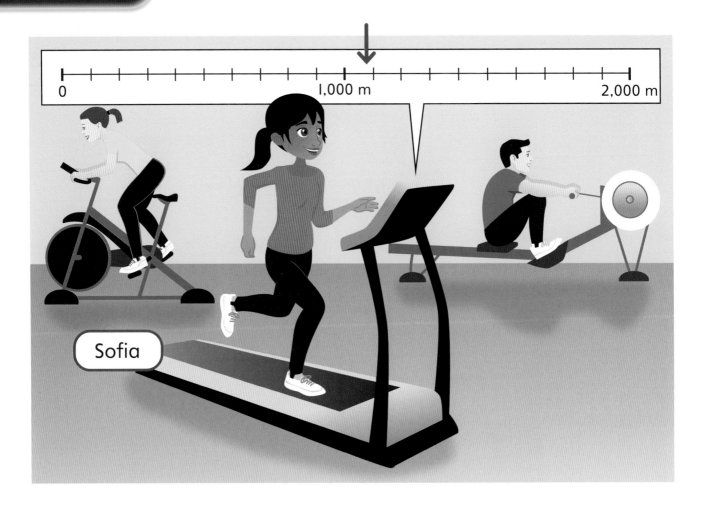

1 **a)** Complete the sentence:

Sofia has run between ⬚ m and ⬚ m.

b) Estimate the distance she has run.

Share

a)

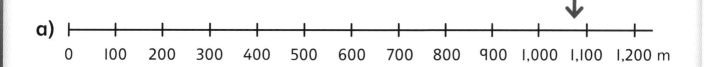

The arrow points **between** two multiples of 100.

Sofia has run between 1,000 m and 1,100 m.

> I think she has run between 1,000 m and 2,000 m.

b) To make a good estimate, zoom in!

Look more closely between the two multiples of 100.

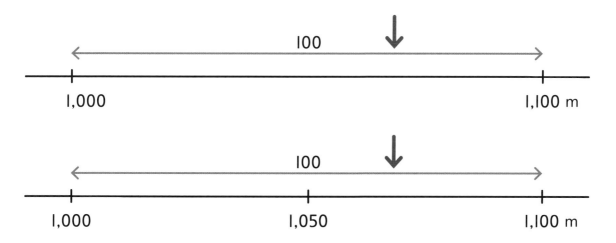

The arrow is past half-way. A good estimate is 1,070 m.

Think together

① What number is exactly in the middle of each number line?

Say a number in section A and a number in section B.

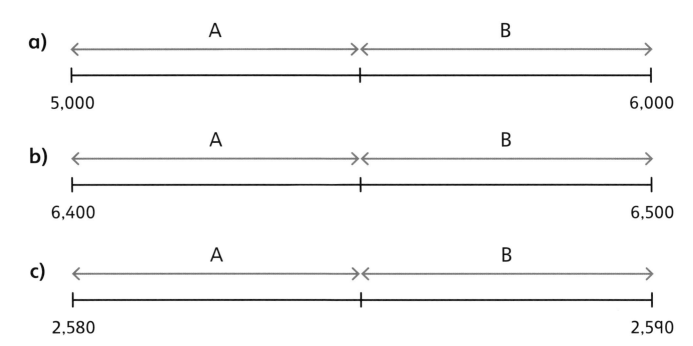

a)

A   B

5,000   6,000

b)

A   B

6,400   6,500

c)

A   B

2,580   2,590

② Sofia uses a bike. The arrow shows how far she has cycled.

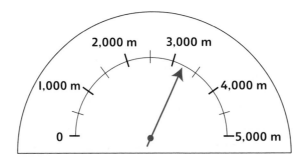

Make a reasonable estimate of the distance.

3 **a)** Sofia rows 8,990 m on the rowing machine.

Point to this distance on each of the scales.

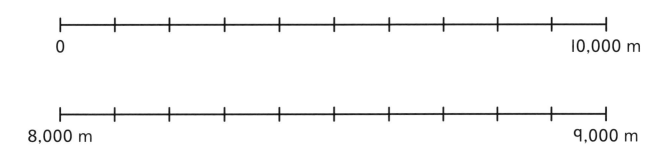

0   10,000 m

8,000 m   9,000 m

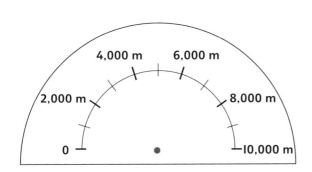

I wonder what 8,990 is close to. This might help me to work out where the number lies.

b) Show the following distances on different number lines or measuring scales.

3,001 m   5,900 m   7,500 m

55

Compare and order numbers to 10,000

Discover

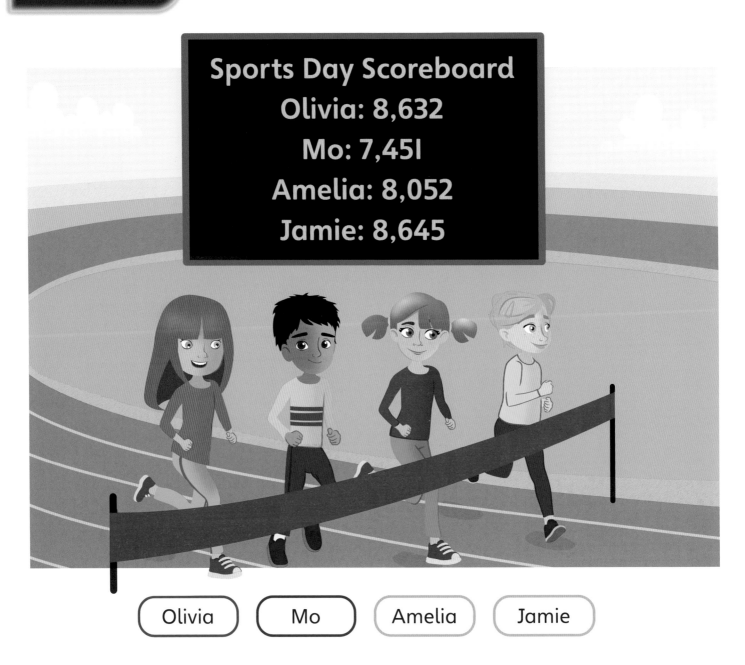

1 a) Who has scored the fewest points so far?

b) Order the top three scores from greatest to fewest number of points.

Share

I compared the numbers in a place value grid.

a)

Name	Th	H	T	O
Olivia	8	6	3	2
Mo	7	4	5	1
Amelia	8	0	5	2
Jamie	8	6	4	5

7,451 has the fewest 1,000s so it is the smallest number.

Mo has scored the fewest points.

b)

Name	Th	H	T	O
Olivia	8	6	3	2
Amelia	8	0	5	2
Jamie	8	6	4	5

8,052 has the fewest 100s so Amelia came 3rd.

All the numbers have 8 thousands.
I looked at the 100s and then the 10s.

Name	Th	H	T	O
Olivia	8	6	3	2
Jamie	8	6	4	5

8,645 has more 10s so it is greater than 8,632.

Jamie came 1st. Olivia came 2nd.

8,645 > 8,632 > 8,052

Think together

1 Compare the numbers.

Th	H	T	O
8	6	2	4
8	4	2	6

☐ is greater than ☐.

☐ ◯ ☐

I wonder how many comparisons I need to make to compare these numbers.

2 | 240 | 1,250 | 1,220 | 1,028 |

a) Write the numbers in ascending order.

☐ < ☐ < ☐ < ☐

b) Now write the numbers in descending order.

☐ > ☐ > ☐ > ☐

3 Discuss how to compare and order these masses.

Tyrannosaurus rex
8,160 kg

Megalosaurus
907 kg

Stegosaurus
2,722 kg

Triceratops
6,350 kg

Ankylosaurus
6,040 kg

0 1,000 2,000 3,000 4,000 5,000 6,000 7,000 8,000 9,000 10,000

I wonder if a 3-digit number is always less than a 4-digit number.

I can think of a number line. The higher the number, the further it is along the number line.

59

→ Practice book 4A p41

Round to the nearest 1,000

Discover

1 **a)** Complete this statement.

   5,275 is between ☐,000 and ☐,000.

b) Use a number line to find which multiple of one thousand 5,275 is closer to.

Share

a) 5,275 is between 5,000 and 6,000.

Previous thousand		Next thousand
[5,000]	5,275	[6,000]

b) 5,500 is the half-way point between 5,000 and 6,000.

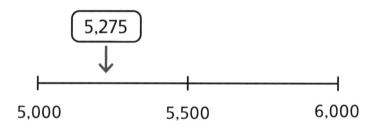

5,275 is closer to 5,000 than 6,000.

> I found the half-way point to help me find the closest multiple.

> You can say 5,275 **rounds** to 5,000, to the nearest 1,000.

The closest multiple of 1,000 is 5,000.

Think together

1 Round 2,891 to the nearest multiple of 1,000.

I think I first need to find the previous and next multiples of 1,000.

I will estimate its position on a number line.

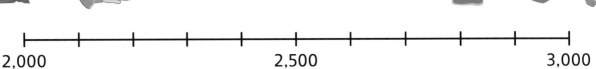

2,000   2,500   3,000

2 Round each number to the nearest multiple of 1,000.

a) 6,200

Previous 1,000   Next 1,000

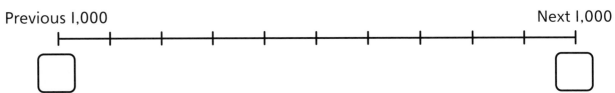

b) 3,760

Previous 1,000   Next 1,000

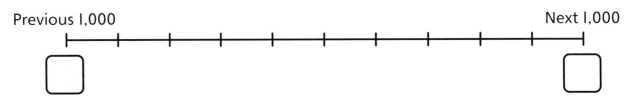

c) 862

Previous 1,000   Next 1,000

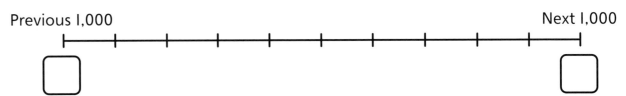

3 Round each number to the nearest 1,000.

2,470   2,883   7,500   3,782   9,501

If a number rounds to the previous multiple, we say it **rounds down**.

If it rounds to the next multiple, we say it **rounds up**.

First, I work out the half-way number between two multiples of 1,000.

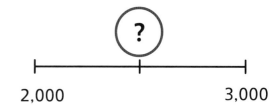

?

2,000   3,000

I think I can see whether to round up or down by thinking about the 100s digit.

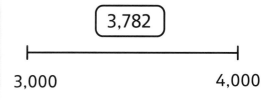

3,782

3,000   4,000

I wonder whether you round up or down if the number is exactly half-way.

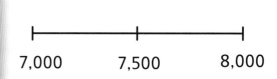

7,000   7,500   8,000

63

→ **Practice book 4A p44**

Round to the nearest 100

Discover

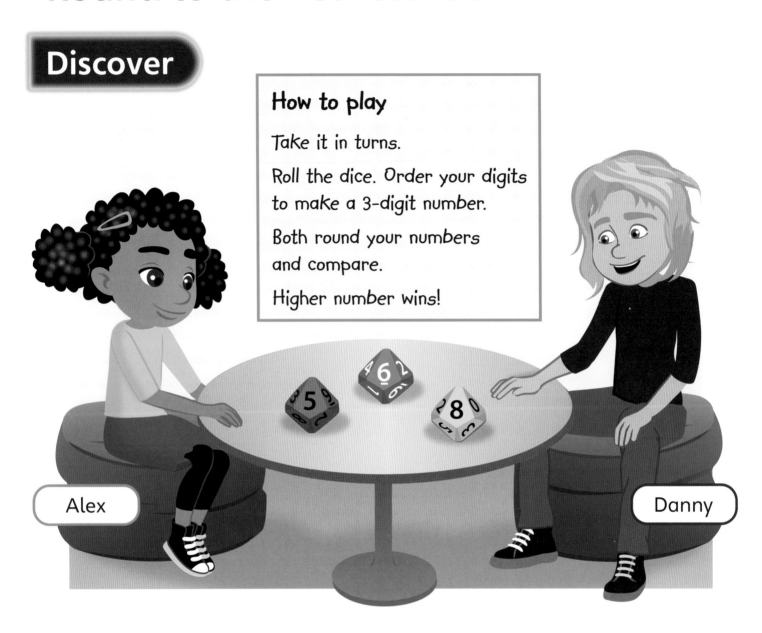

How to play

Take it in turns.

Roll the dice. Order your digits to make a 3-digit number.

Both round your numbers and compare.

Higher number wins!

Alex

Danny

1 a) Danny rolls 568. Complete this sentence:

568 is between ☐00 and ☐00.

b) Round 568 to the nearest multiple of 100.

Share

a) 568 is between 500 and 600.

Previous hundred   Next hundred

500   568   600

550 is the half-way point between 500 and 600.

b)

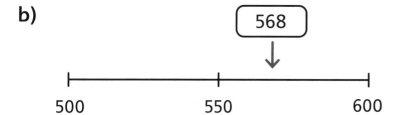

568 is past the half-way point, so it rounds **up** to the next multiple.

The closest multiple of 100 is 600.

Think together

1 Round each number to the nearest 100.

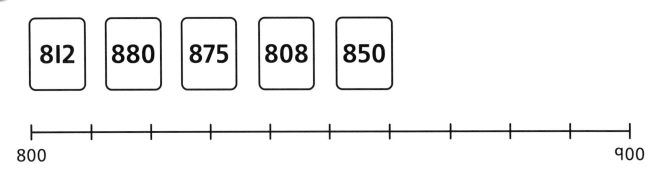

2 Round each number to the nearest multiple of 100.

a) 4,595

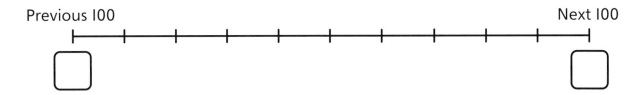

b) 2,340

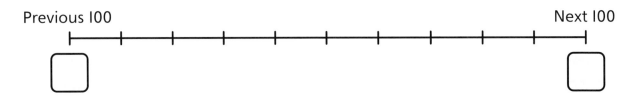

c) 1,050

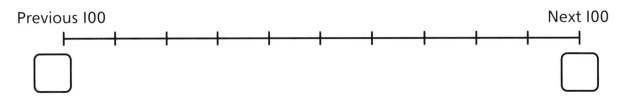

CHALLENGE

3 Choose one list.

List A	List B	List C
503	2,402	547
513	2,412	1,547
523	2,422	2,547
533	2,432	3,547
543	2,442	4,547
553	2,452	5,547
563	2,462	6,547
573	2,472	7,547
583	2,482	8,547
593	2,492	9,547

Round each number in the list to the nearest 100.

Discuss what you notice.

I'm going to draw number lines to explore how this works.

67

→ Practice book 4A p47

Round to the nearest 10

Discover

1 a) Which numbers are closer to 20?

Which numbers are closer to 30?

b) Round each number to the nearest multiple of 10.

Share

a) These numbers are closer to 20.

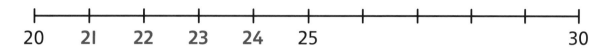

These numbers are closer to 30.

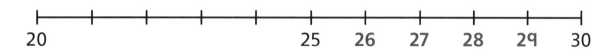

I would have to add 6 to 24 to reach 30, but subtract only 4 to reach 20.

b)

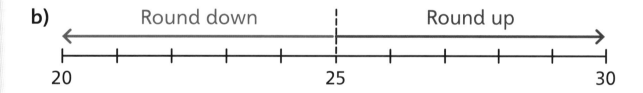

25 is exactly half-way between 20 and 30. It rounds up to 30.

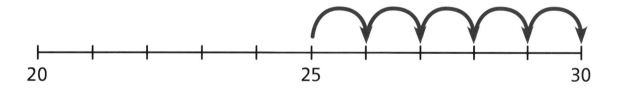

If there are 5 or more Is, you round up to the next I0.

69

Think together

1   Round each number to the nearest 10.

a)   32

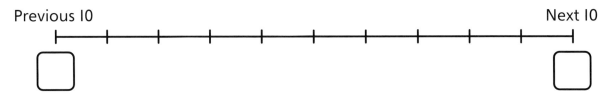

b)   167

c)   1,278

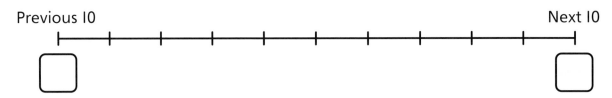

2   Complete the table.

Animal	Number	Rounded to nearest 10
birds	176	180
lizards	48	☐
fish	131	☐
monkeys	40	☐
snakes	☐	60

I will try to find all possible answers for the number of snakes.

CHALLENGE

3 Pick two digit cards to make a 2-digit number.

| 3 | 5 | 1 | 7 |

Challenge your partner to round it to the nearest 10.

I wonder if there's a quick way to think about the numbers.

I can tell whether to round up or down by looking at the 1s digit.

Now play this game by making 3-digit and 4-digit numbers.

Challenge a partner to round your number to the nearest 10 by thinking about the 1s.

71

→ **Practice book 4A p50**

Round to the nearest 1,000, 100 or 10

Discover

4,000 g   5,000 g

1 **a)** Estimate the position of 4,949 g on the measuring scale.

   b) Round 4,949 to the nearest 1,000, 100 and 10.

Share

a) You can use a number line.

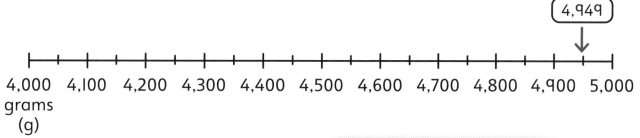

4,000 4,100 4,200 4,300 4,400 4,500 4,600 4,700 4,800 4,900 5,000
grams
(g)

> I checked what each interval on the number line represents.

b) You can round the same number to the nearest 1,000, 100 or 10. Rounding to the nearest 10 is the most accurate.

Previous thousand   Next thousand

4,000   4,949   5,000 ⟶ Rounds up to 5,000

Previous hundred   Next hundred

4,900   4,949   5,000 ⟶ Rounds down to 4,900

Previous ten   Next ten

4,940   4,949   4,950 ⟶ Rounds up to 4,950

73

Think together

1 Round 3,511 to the nearest 10, 100 and 1,000.

Rounded to nearest	10	100	1,000
3,511			

2 What is the smallest number that rounds to 2,000?

☐ is the smallest number that rounds to 2,000

What is the greatest number that rounds to 2,000?

☐ is the greatest number that rounds to 2,000

This must mean rounding to the nearest 1,000.

2,000 is also a multiple of 100 and of 10 … so I think there are more solutions.

74

CHALLENGE

3 Discuss different methods for rounding.

Th	H	T	O
3	7	2	5

I look at the 100s digit to see whether to round up or down.

I work out the previous and next multiples.

I wonder which is the best method.

I draw a number line each time I round.

→ **Practice book 4A p53**

End of unit check

1 What number is the arrow pointing to?

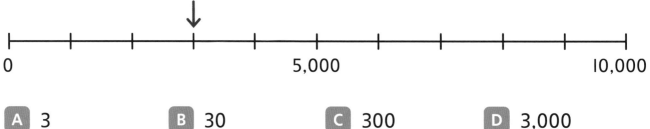

A 3   B 30   C 300   D 3,000

2 Round the following to the nearest 1,000.

Th	H	T	O
●●●●● ●●●●	●●●●●●	●●●●●	

A 9,550   B 9,500   C 9,000   D 10,000

3 Which of these numbers round to 3,100 to the nearest 100?

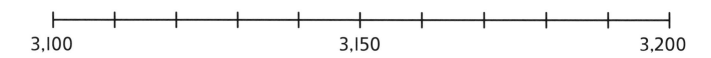

A 3,150   B 2,999   C 3,020   D 3,134

4 What sign is missing to make the statement correct?

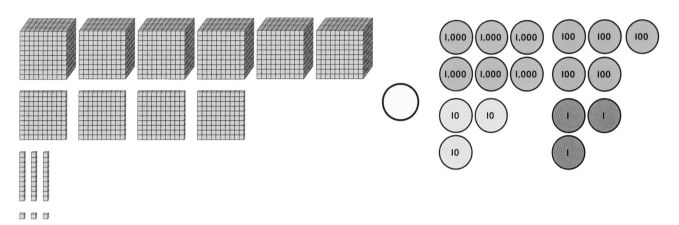

A < 　　　　　 B > 　　　　　 C = 　　　　　 D £

5 The mass of 4 boxes are shown.

Which box is the lightest?

A 345 g 　　　　 B 98 g 　　　　 C 1,007 g 　　　　 D 820 g

6 Round these numbers to the nearest 10, 100 and 1,000.

Rounded to nearest	10	100	1,000
858			
2,605			

→ **Practice book 4A p56**

Unit 3
Addition and subtraction

In this unit we will …

⚡ Add and subtract Is, 10s, 100s and 1,000s

⚡ Add and subtract two 4-digit numbers using the column method

⚡ Learn how to find and use equivalent difference, and other mental methods

⚡ Estimate answers to additions and subtractions

⚡ Learn how to check strategies and apply our knowledge

Do you remember what this is called? We use it to compare amounts.

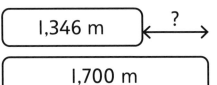

1,346 m ⟷ ?

1,700 m

We will need some maths words. Do you know what they all mean?

addition   total   more than

subtraction   less than   column method

estimate   how much   strategy

efficient   accurate   exact   fact

We need to use the part-whole model too. It helps us to break down and solve problems.

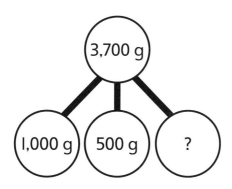

3,700 g

1,000 g   500 g   ?

Add and subtract 1s, 10s, 100s, 1,000s

Discover

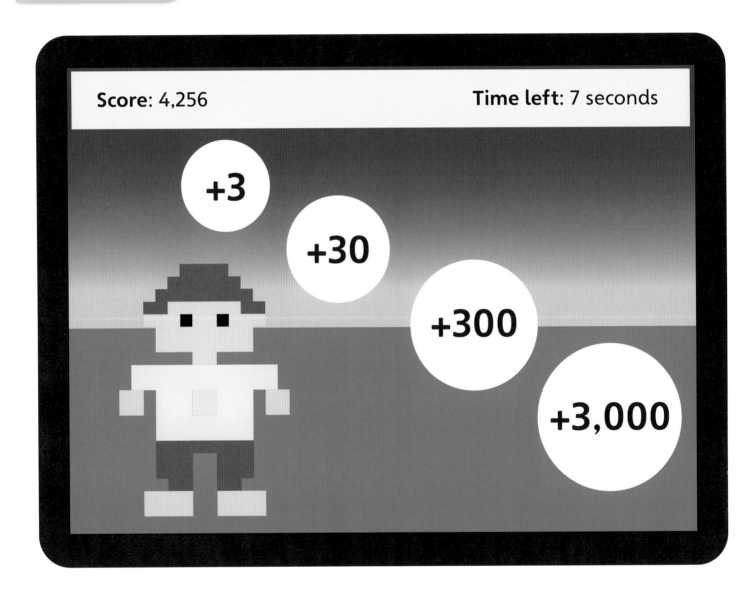

1 a) Make Reena's score of 4,256 with place value counters.

b) Show how Reena's score will change if she catches another bubble.

Share

> I can tell which digit is going to change.

a)

Th	H	T	O
1,000 1,000 1,000 1,000	100 100	10 10 10 10 10	● ● ● ● ● ●

b)

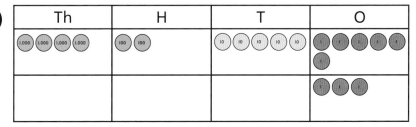

$$4,256 + 3 = 4,259$$

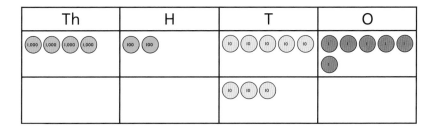

$$4,256 + 30 = 4,286$$

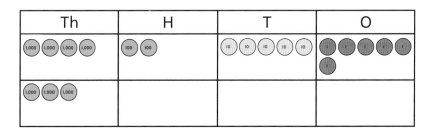

$$4,256 + 300 = 4,556$$

Th	H	T	O
1,000 1,000 1,000 1,000	100 100	10 10 10 10 10	● ● ● ● ● ●
1,000 1,000 1,000			

$$4,256 + 3,000 = 7,256$$

Think together

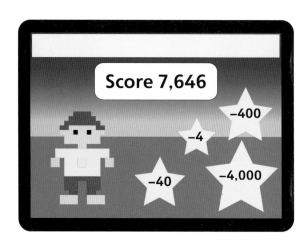

1 Ellie's score is 7,646.

Th	H	T	O

How would each star change Ellie's score?

a)

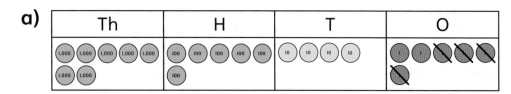

$7,646 - 4 = \square$

b)

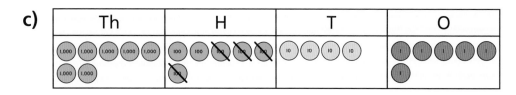

$7,646 - 40 = \square$

c)

Th	H	T	O

$7,646 - 400 = \square$

d)

Th	H	T	O

$7,646 - 4,000 = \square$

2 Lewis has scored 8,888. Show how his score would change each time.

a) $8,888 - 500 = \square$

c) $\square = 8,888 - 5,000$

b) $8,888 - \square = 8,883$

d) $8,838 = 8,888 - \square$

82

3 **a)** Max has scored 3,869 points.

He hits a +5,000 bubble, then a −2,000 star.

What will his score be now?

I wonder what happens if I do this calculation in a different order.

I will combine the bubble and the star first, to work out how Max's score changes.

b) Jamilla has 4,545 points.

She hits a star, then a bubble.
Now she has 4,555 points.

What star and bubble could she have hit?
Find five possible answers.

→ Practice book 4A p58

Add two 4-digit numbers

Discover

1 **a)** Use place value counters to represent the mass of each piece of luggage.

b) Find the total mass.

Share

a)

Th	H	T	O
1,000 1,000 1,000 1,000	100 100 100 100 100 10 10		● ● ● ●
1,000 1,000 1,000	100 100 100 100	10 10 10	●

b) Add each column, starting with the 1s.

Th	H	T	O
1,000 1,000 1,000 1,000	100 100 100 100 100 10 10		● ● ● ●
1,000 1,000 1,000	100 100 100 100	10 10 10	●

	Th	H	T	O
		4	5	2	3
+		3	4	3	1
					4

Th	H	T	O
1,000 1,000 1,000 1,000	100 100 100 100 100	10 10	● ● ● ●
1,000 1,000 1,000	100 100 100 100	10 10 10	●

	Th	H	T	O
		4	5	2	3
+		3	4	3	1
				5	4

Th	H	T	O
1,000 1,000 1,000 1,000	100 100 100 100 100	10 10	● ● ●
1,000 1,000 1,000	100 100 100 100	10 10 10	●

	Th	H	T	O
		4	5	2	3
+		3	4	3	1
			9	5	4

Th	H	T	O
1,000 1,000 1,000 1,000	100 100 100 100 100	10 10	● ● ●
1,000 1,000 1,000	100 100 100 100	10 10 10	●

	Th	H	T	O
		4	5	2	3
+		3	4	3	1
	7	9	5	4

4,523 + 3,431 = 7,954. The total mass is 7,954 g.

Think together

1 What is the total mass of the two bags?

Th	H	T	O
1,000 1,000 1,000	100	10 10 10 10	1 1

Th	H	T	O
1,000 1,000	100 100 100		1 1 1 1 1 1 1

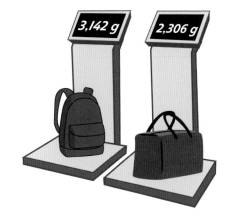

3,142 g   2,306 g

Th	H	T	O
	3	1	4	2
+	2	3	0	6

2 Use place value equipment to show the mistake that Kate has made.

Th	H	T	O
	4	5	2	1
+	3	4	6	
	7	9	8	1

I made sure the digits lined up.

Kate

4,521 + 346 = 7,981

86

CHALLENGE

3 The total mass of two suitcases is 7,777 g.

The mass of the first suitcase is 3,452 g.

What is the mass of the second suitcase?

Th	H	T	O
1,000 1,000 1,000	100 100 100 100	10 10 10 10 10	1 1
1,000 1,000 1,000 1,000 1,000 1,000 1,000	100 100 100 100 100 100 100	10 10 10 10 10 10 10	1 1 1 1 1 1 1

	Th	H	T	O
	3	4	5	2
+				
	7	7	7	7

I will use my number bonds.

I will use counters and work out **how much** to add to each column.

87

Add two 4-digit numbers – one exchange

Discover

We will fly from Istanbul to London, then from London to Nairobi.

Flight information

MONDAY

Istanbul to London:
1,554 miles

London to Nairobi:
4,237 miles

1 a) Represent the two distances using place value counters.

What do you notice about the number of 1s counters?

b) What is the total distance that the plane will fly?

Share

a)

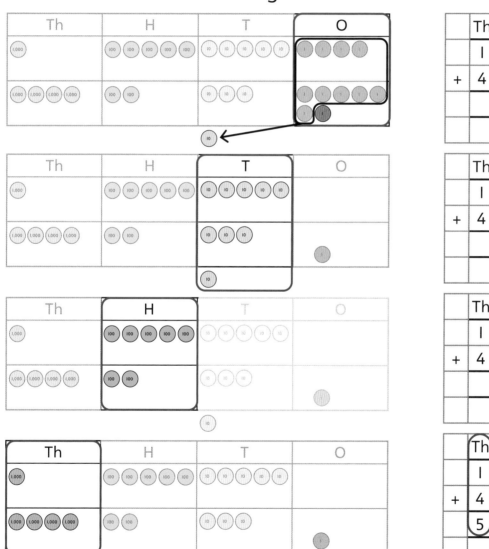

The 1s add up to more than 10.

b) This addition has an exchange from the 1s to the 10s.

Th	H	T	O
	1	5	5	4

The plane will fly 5,791 miles in total.

Think together

1 On Monday a plane flies 5,791 miles.

On Tuesday it flies 1,154 miles further than on Monday.

How far does the plane fly on Tuesday?

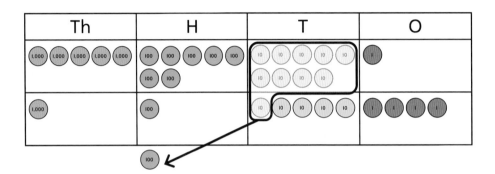

Th	H	T	O
	5	7	9	1
+	1	1	5	4

2 Choose a number to complete this addition story problem so that there will be an exchange from the 100s to the 1,000s.

A plane flies on Wednesday and Thursday.

It flies 3,201 miles on Thursday.

How many miles does it fly in total?

Now complete your calculation.

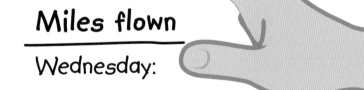

Miles flown

Wednesday:

Thursday: 3,201 miles

Th	H	T	O
+	3	2	0	1

CHALLENGE

3 **a)** Match each addition to the correct exchange description.

$2,341 + 1,593 = \boxed{}$ $1,010 + 2,549 = \boxed{}$

$\boxed{} = 6,917 + 782$ $\boxed{} = 2,001 + 9$

| no exchange needed | exchange 10 ones | exchange 10 tens | exchange 10 hundreds |

Now complete the additions.

I will write each of them in columns.

I think a mental **strategy** is better for two of these.

b) Choose one of the additions.

Write two different story problems for this addition.

→ **Practice book 4A p64**

Add with more than one exchange

Discover

Sports car £4,799

Motorbike £1,099

Van £1,909

Vintage car £775

1 **a)** Find the total cost of the sports car and the vintage car.

b) Find the total cost of the motorbike, the van and the vintage car.

Share

a)

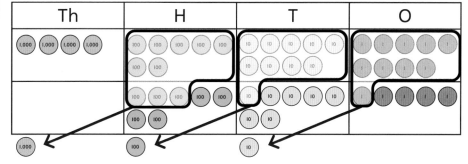

	Th	H	T	O
		4	7	9	9
+			7	7	5
		5	5	7	4
		1	1	1	

The total cost of the sports car and the vintage car is £5,574.

b) Add the columns, starting with the 1s.

	Th	H	T	O
		1	9	0	9
		1	0	9	9
+				7	7	5
		3	7	8	3
		1	1	2	

The total cost of the motorbike, the van and the vintage car is £3,783.

You need to exchange 20 ones for 2 tens.

Think together

1 How much do the van and the vintage car cost in total?

Vintage car
£775

Van
£1,909

Th	H	T	O
1,000	100 100 100 100 100		1 1 1 1 1 1
	100 100 100 100		1 1 1 1 1
	100 100 100 100 100	10 10 10 10 10	1 1 1 1 1 1
	100 100	10 10	

	Th	H	T	O
		1	9	0	9
+			7	7	5

I need to think carefully about how to write the addition in columns.

2 **a)** The caravan costs £1,775 more than the motorbike.

How much does the caravan cost?

b) How much do the caravan and motorbike cost altogether?

Motorbike
£1,099

	Th	H	T	O
+		1	7	7	5

	Th	H	T	O
+					

3 **a)** Find the missing digits to add to the next multiple of 1,000.

	Th	H	T	O
	1	2	5	9
+				
	2	0	0	0

	Th	H	T	O
			6	3
+	2			7
	3	0	0	0

	Th	H	T	O
	4		6	
+		9		9
	5	0	0	0

	Th	H	T	O
			8	8
+	8	8		
	9	0	0	0

b) Work out the size of each jump.

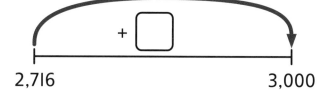

2,716   3,000

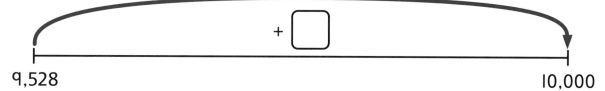

9,528   10,000

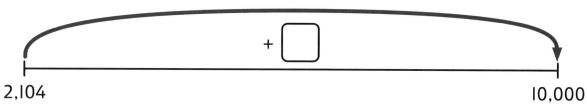

2,104   10,000

95

Subtract two 4-digit numbers

Discover

1 **a)** Decimal Pointers want to know how many votes they got.
Show how they could work this out using a bar model.

b) How many votes did Decimal Pointers get?

Share

a)

Total votes
5,432

?	1,312

Decimal Pointers   Make That

I did a subtraction to work out the missing part.

b)

	Th	H	T	O
	1,000 1,000 1,000 1,000 1,000	100 100 100 100	10 10 10	⊘⊘

	Th	H	T	O
	5	4	3	2
−	1	3	1	2
				0

	Th	H	T	O
	1,000 1,000 1,000 1,000 1,000	100 100 100 100	10 10 ⊘	⊘⊘

	Th	H	T	O
	5	4	3	2
−	1	3	1	2
			2	0

	Th	H	T	O
	1,000 1,000 1,000 1,000 1,000	100 ⊘ ⊘ ⊘	10 10 ⊘	⊘⊘

	Th	H	T	O
	5	4	3	2
−	1	3	1	2
		1	2	0

	Th	H	T	O
	1,000 1,000 1,000 1,000 ⊘	100 ⊘ ⊘ ⊘	10 10 ⊘	⊘⊘

	Th	H	T	O
	5	4	3	2
−	1	3	1	2
	4	1	2	0

5,432 − 1,312 = 4,120

Decimal Pointers got 4,120 votes.

Think together

1 Angle Anderson got 4,324 votes.

Scissor Squares got 2,120 fewer votes than Angle Anderson.

How many votes did Scissor Squares get?

Th	H	T	O
1,000 1,000 1,000 1,000	100 100 100	10 10	1 1 1 1

	Th	H	T	O
		4	3	2	4
−				

2 Work out the missing number in 5,465 − ☐ = 5,201.

Th	H	T	O
1,000 1,000 1,000 1,000 1,000	100 100 100 100	10 10 10 10 10 10	1 1 1 1 1 1

	Th	H	T	O
		5	4	6	5
−				
		5	2	0	1

I will write out the full calculation to check.

3 **a)** Use subtraction to work out the missing numbers in these models.

9,876	
5,432	?

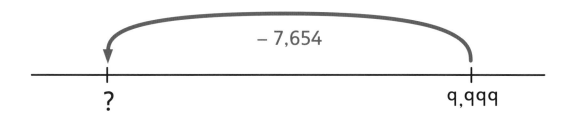

$- 7,654$

?   9,999

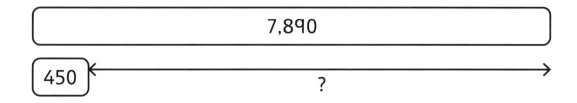

7,890

450   ?

b) Draw your own models to represent the subtraction 7,654 − 4,321 in different ways.

I will draw a part-whole model.

99

→ **Practice book 4A p70**

Subtract two 4-digit numbers – one exchange

Discover

	Th	H	T	O
	1	2	5	0
−		3	2	0
	1	1	3	0

I think I will have 1,130 ml of orange juice left.

Fruit punch
- 320 ml of orange juice
- Fruit pieces

1,250 ml

Aki

1 **a)** Explain the mistake that Aki has made in his calculation.

b) How much orange juice will Aki have left?

Share

a)

Th	H	T	O
	1	2	5	0
−		3	2	0
	1	1	3	0

The calculation shows
2 – 3, not 3 – 2.

In the hundreds column, Aki has subtracted 2 hundreds from 3 hundreds, but he needed to exchange and then take 3 away from 12.

b)

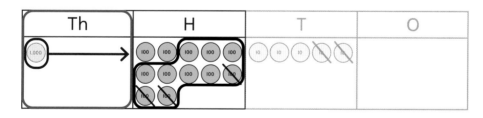

	Th	H	T	O
		1	2	5	0
−			3	2	0
					0

	Th	H	T	O
		1	2	5	0
−			3	2	0
				3	0

	Th	H	T	O
	𝟙̸	¹2	5	0
−			3	2	0
		9	3	0

	Th	H	T	O
	𝟙̸	¹2	5	0
−			3	2	0
		9	3	0

1,250 − 320 = 930. Aki will have 930 ml of orange juice left.

Think together

1 Aki had 1,750 ml of mango juice, but he spilled some.

Now he has 625 ml.

How much did he spill?

Th	H	T	O
1,000	100 100 100 100 100 100 100	10 10 10 10 10	

	Th	H	T	O
	1	7	5	0
−		6	2	5

2 Lee and Mo are playing a computer game.

Lee scores 1,725 points.

Mo scores 1,175 points.

NEW SCORE
Lee   1,725
Mo   1,175

Lee

Mo

How many more points did Lee score than Mo?

3 What digits have been covered?

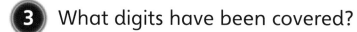

	Th	H	T	O
	3	2	5	3
−	2	1	✹	6
	1	1	2	✹

	Th	H	T	O
	4	2	3	6
−	2	✹	2	✹
	1	5	✹	3

	Th	H	T	O
	6	7	2	9
−	✹	✹	✹	✹
	3	3	3	3

	Th	H	T	O
	✹	✹	✹	✹
−	2	1	2	7
	6	4	3	8

I will think about what I can do to check my answers.

I wonder if I can just use my number bonds.

103

→ Practice book 4A p73

Subtract two 4-digit numbers – more than one exchange

Discover

I have saved £1,450.

Large screen TV £2,450

TV £1,295

Tablet £549

Laptop £849

Jen

1 **a)** Jen buys a laptop.

How many exchanges does she need to make to work out this calculation?

£1,450 – £849?

b) How much money does she have left?

Share

a) 1,450 – 849

I think this needs two exchanges.

I started with the Is and checked for exchanges as I went.

Th	H	T	O
1	4	⁴5̶	¹0
–	8	4	9
			1

Th	H	T	O
1	4	⁴5̶	¹0
–	8	4	9
		0	1

Th	H	T	O
1̶	¹4	⁴5̶	¹0
–		8	4	9
	6	0	1

Th	H	T	O
1̶	¹4	⁴5̶	¹0
–		8	4	9
	6	0	1

Jen needs to make 2 exchanges.

b) 1,450 – 849 = 601

Jen has £601 left.

Think together

1 What is the difference in price between the two televisions?

> Sometimes you will need to exchange into a column that you have already exchanged out of.

> I will make sure to write the subtraction carefully so each exchange is clear!

	Th		H			T				O	
	1,000 1,000		100 100 100 100			10 10 10 10 10					

	Th	H	T	O
		2	4	5	0
−	1	2	9	5

2 Calculate the missing part.

£2,450

£1,880	?

	Th	H	T	O
−				

3 **a)** In a sale, there is £199 off the price of a small television.

How much does it cost now?

I think I'm only going to have to make an exchange in the 1s to work this out.

Th	H	T	O
	1	2	9	5
–		1	9	9

Complete the calculation.

Is Astrid correct? Explain your answer.

b) Make up three more calculations that need more than one exchange.

I will make up calculations with one, two and three exchanges.

I wonder if I can make up a calculation with four exchanges.

107

→ Practice book 4A p76

Exchange across two columns

Discover

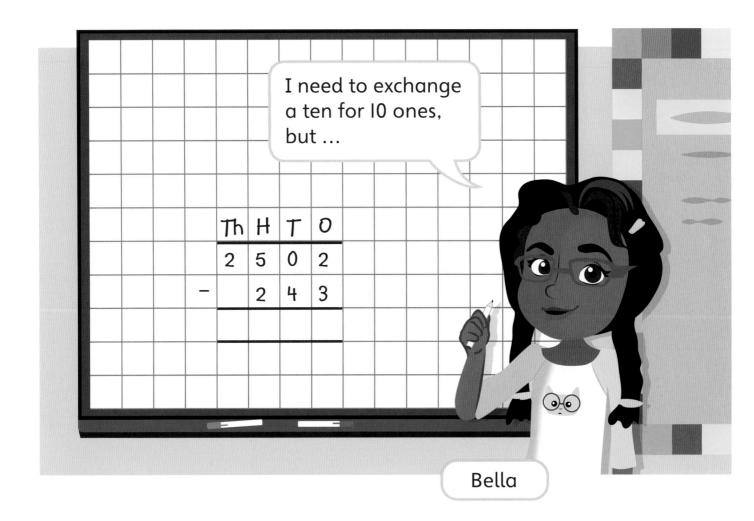

I need to exchange a ten for 10 ones, but …

Th	H	T	O
2	5	0	2
−	2	4	3

Bella

1 **a)** Why is Bella confused?

What advice would you give her?

b) Complete Bella's subtraction.

Share

a) Bella wants to exchange a ten for 10 ones, but she cannot because 2,502 doesn't have any 10s.

> When I am stuck, I use equipment to show the problem.

First, Bella should exchange 1 hundred for 10 tens.

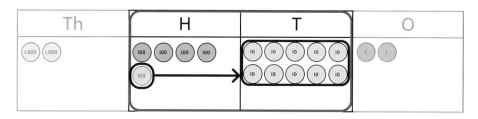

Th	H	T	O
2	⁴5̶ ¹0	2	
−		2	4	3

Then she can exchange 1 ten for 10 ones.

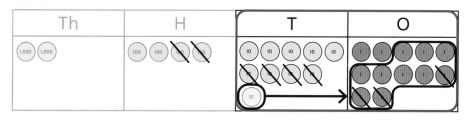

Th	H	T	O
2	⁴5̶	⁹1̶0̶	¹2
−		2	4	3

b) Now Bella can subtract the 1s and complete the subtraction.

Th	H	T	O
2	⁴5̶	⁹1̶0̶	¹2
−		2	4	3
2	2	5	9

2,502 − 243 = 2,259

Think together

1 Complete the subtractions.

a) 2,032 – 512 = ☐

Th	H	T	O
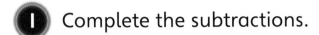		10 10 10	● ●

	Th	H	T	O
	2	0	3	2
–		5	1	2

b) 5,403 – 505 = ☐

Th	H	T	O
1,000 1,000 1,000 1,000 1,000	100 100 100 100		● ● ●

	Th	H	T	O
	5	4	0	3
–		5	0	5

I think I will need to make more than one exchange to do the subtraction in one of the columns.

2 Zac has worked out 3,304 − 1,269.

Th	H	T	O
3	3	ʹ0	ʹ4
− 1	2	6	9
2	1	4	5

Explain the mistakes Zac has made.

Correct his calculation.

3 Predict the exchanges you will need to make, then complete the subtractions to check.

☐ = 5,055 − 2,929

☐ = 5,505 − 2,929

☐ = 5,005 − 2,929

☐ = 5,005 − 2,525

I will use place value equipment to show the exchanges and explain my predictions.

111

Efficient methods

Discover

1,517 + 999

1,517 − 999

1 **a)** Solve each calculation using a column method.

b) Discuss other possible methods to solve these calculations.

Share

a) Each column method has many exchanges.

	Th	H	T	O
	1	5	1	7
+		9	9	9
	2	5	1	6
		1	1	1

	Th	H	T	O
	¹⁴X	¹⁴5̸	¹⁰X̸	¹7
–		9	9	9
		5	1	8

b) A number line is another possible method.

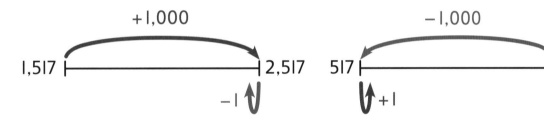

$$1,517 + 1,000 = 2,517$$

$$1,517 + 999 = 2,516$$

$$1,517 - 1,000 = 517$$

$$1,517 - 999 = 518$$

I think there are other methods I can use.

Think together

1 **a)** Solve the addition using a written and a mental method.

$$1,999 + 575 = \boxed{}$$

> 1,999 is very close to 2,000.

> One of these numbers only has three digits.

> I think this will have three exchanges.

> I think I can solve this mentally.

Which method do you prefer? Why?

b) Write some more additions that can be solved mentally like this.

2 Complete each calculation.

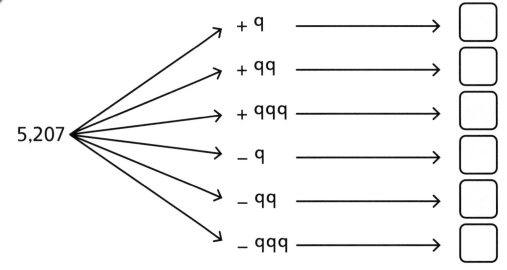

5,207

+ 9 ⟶ ☐

+ 99 ⟶ ☐

+ 999 ⟶ ☐

– 9 ⟶ ☐

– 99 ⟶ ☐

– 999 ⟶ ☐

3 **a)** Use the different methods to complete the calculations.

2,001 – 1,998   2,001 – 5

	Th	H	T	O
	2	0	0	1
–	1	9	9	8

	Th	H	T	O
	2	0	0	1
–				5

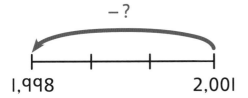

– ?

1,998   2,001

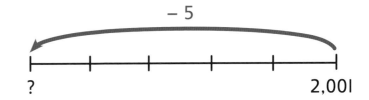

– 5

?   2,001

2,001

1,998

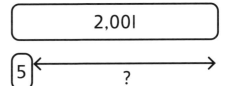

2,001

5   ?

b) Complete the calculations mentally.

2,991 – 2   = ☐

2,001 – 9   = ☐

1,001 – 999 = ☐

What method did you use?

Compare with a partner.

I use different methods depending on the numbers.

115

→ Practice book 4A p82

Equivalent difference

Discover

I am 96 years old today.

I am 8 years old today.

Great-grandad

Amelia

1 **a)** Amelia says that when her great-grandad is 100, there will be even more years between their ages than there are now.

Show whether this is true or not.

b) What will be the difference between their ages when Amelia's great-grandad is 100?

Share

I showed this using two bars.
Every time her great-grandad
has a birthday, Amelia will too.

a)

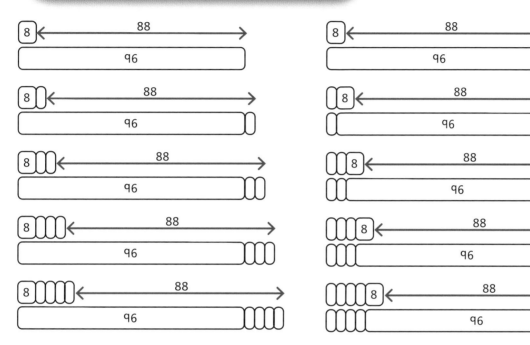

The difference between their ages will always be the same.

b) All of these subtractions give the difference between their ages.

	T	O
	9	6
−		8

	T	O
	9	7
−		9

	T	O
	9	8
−	1	0
	8	8

	T	O
	9	9
−	1	1
	8	8

	H	T	O
	1	0	0
−		1	2

The two subtractions without exchanges are the quickest to
work out. 98 – 10 = 88 and 99 – 11 = 88.

When her great-grandad is 100, Amelia will be 12.
The difference between their ages will still be 88 years.

Think together

1 An apple tree is 79 years old and an oak tree is 198 years old.

Write a different subtraction for each bar model.

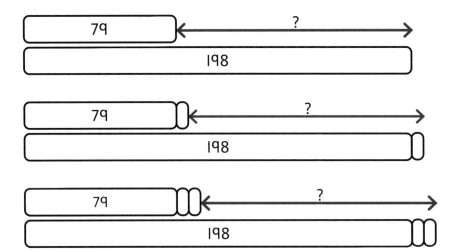

	H	T	O
	1	9	8
−		7	9

Choose one of the subtractions to find the difference between the ages of the two trees, and then complete all of the subtractions.

2 A giant tortoise is 125 years old and a whale is 97 years old.

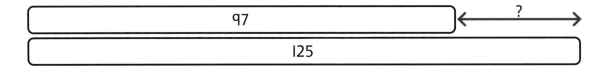

Write some subtractions for when they are different ages and choose one to find the difference.

	H	T	O
	1	2	5
−		9	7

	H	T	O
	1	2	6
−		9	8

	H	T	O
−			

	H	T	O
−			

	H	T	O
−			

3 **a)** 1,000 − 245 = ☐

CHALLENGE

I will do this as a column subtraction. First, I will need to exchange 1 thousand for 10 hundreds.

I will just work out 999 − 244.

Which method do you think is better?
Why do you think so?

Now try both methods and compare them.

Th	H	T	O
1	0	0	0
−		2	4	5

Th	H	T	O
	9	9	9
−		2	4	4

Which is more **efficient**?

b) Find efficient ways to solve these subtractions.

1,000 − 542   2,001 − 265

2,692 − 836   1,897 − 999

I wonder if I should use the same way for all of these subtractions.

119

→ **Practice book 4A p85**

Estimate answers

Discover

1 **a)** Is this an **accurate** estimate?

b) Check if the estimate is close to the **exact** calculation.

Share

a)

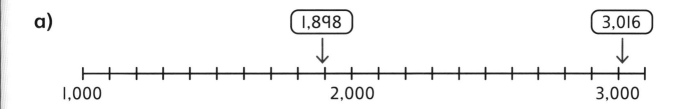

1,898 is closer to 2,000 than 1,000.

A better estimate would be
2,000 + 3,000 = 5,000.

They have sold roughly 5,000 tickets.

I rounded 1,898 and 3,016 to the nearest 1,000.

b)

Th	H	T	O
3	0	1	6
+ 1	8	9	8
4	9	1	4
		1	1

The exact answer is 4,914 tickets.

4,914 rounds to 5,000.

5,000 is a better estimate than 4,000.

I wonder what estimate I would make if I rounded to the nearest 100.

Think together

1 At a theatre, there were 6,149 people in the audience, but 912 of them left during the interval.

Round to the nearest 1,000 to estimate how many people stayed.

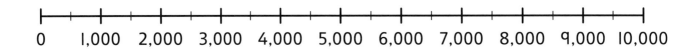

0   1,000   2,000   3,000   4,000   5,000   6,000   7,000   8,000   9,000   10,000

6,149 rounds to ☐,000 to the nearest 1,000.

912 rounds to ☐,000 to the nearest 1,000.

> I can add and subtract these mentally.

Approximately ☐ people stayed.

2 | 2,794 + 3,911 | | 9,811 + 2,788 |

a) Estimate the answer to each calculation by rounding to the nearest 1,000.

b) Estimate the answer to each calculation by rounding to the nearest 100.

c) Now work out the exact answers.

What do you notice?

122

3 Max used a column subtraction to solve

5,602 − 2,975 = ☐

	Th	H	T	O
	⁴5̷	¹⁵6̷	⁹⁄0̷	¹2
−	2	9	7	5
	2	6	2	7

Isla and Aki used estimates to check Max's working.

I rounded 2,975 to 3,000, then worked out
5,602 − 3,000 = 2,602.
I think Max's answer is right.

I rounded both numbers and then worked it out.
6,000 − 3,000 = 3,000.
I think Max's answer is wrong.

Isla

Aki

a) Explain the differences between Isla's way of estimating and the method that Aki used.

b) Which estimate works better?

c) How would an estimate have helped Max?

→ **Practice book 4A p88**

Check strategies

Discover

1 a) How can the astronaut check her calculation?

b) Show two ways to do the calculation.

Share

a) A subtraction can be checked by using the inverse operation, which is addition.

1,225	
799	574

	Th	H	T	O
		7	9	9
+		5	7	4
	1	3	7	3
		₁	₁	₁

I used the fact family to check by adding the parts.

I checked by estimating.

The parts do not match the whole. The astronaut's calculation should be done again.

b)

	Th	H	T	O
	⌀	¹¹2	¹¹2	¹5
–			7	9	9
			4	2	6

	Th	H	T	O
	⌀	¹2	2	6
–			8	0	0
			4	2	6

I found an easier way. I added 1 to each number.

There are 426 km left to travel.

Think together

1 The mass of the astronaut's food has to be calculated accurately.

Check the calculation using the inverse operation.

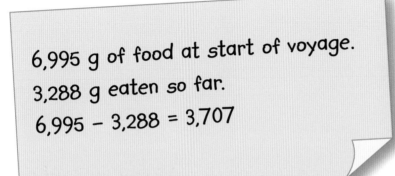

6,995 g of food at start of voyage.

3,288 g eaten so far.

6,995 − 3,288 = 3,707

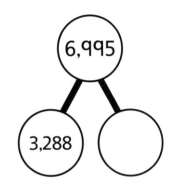

The parts **do** / **do not** match the whole.

The calculation **is** / **is not** correct.

2 Write a calculation to check each of these.

a)

199 + 3,401 = 5,391

b)

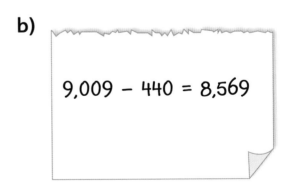

9,009 − 440 = 8,569

Complete any corrections that are needed.

3 Represent each missing number calculation using a part-whole model and a bar model.

$1,090 + \boxed{} = 3,000$

$2,550 = \boxed{} + 1,850$

$4,000 - \boxed{} = 1,250$

$\boxed{} - 750 = 2,000$

Now choose a calculation to find each of the missing numbers.

Use inverse operations to check your answers.

I wonder if a part-whole model or a bar model shows the numbers best.

I think it helps to draw a diagram with parts and wholes to show the missing information.

127

Problem solving – one step

Discover

1 a) Show how to find the number of votes for Yes using a diagram.

b) Decide on the best strategy to calculate the answer.

Did Yes or No get more votes?

Share

a)

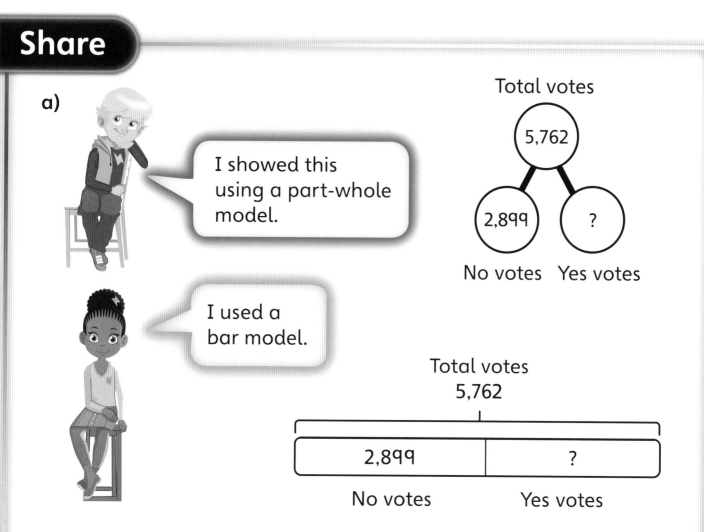

I showed this using a part-whole model.

Total votes

5,762

2,899   ?

No votes   Yes votes

I used a bar model.

Total votes
5,762

2,899	?

No votes   Yes votes

Both models show the parts and the whole.

The missing part is the number of Yes votes.

b) We need to subtract to find the missing part.

Th	H	T	O
⁴5̶	¹⁶7̶	¹⁵6̶	¹2
− 2	8	9	9
2	8	6	3

Th	H	T	O
⁴5̶	¹7	6	3
− 2	9	0	0
2	8	6	3

There were **2,863** Yes votes.

No got more votes because 2,899 > 2,863.

Think together

1 In another vote, 1,775 people voted yes and 3,007 voted No.

How many people voted?

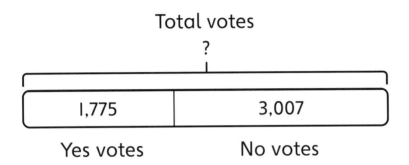

2 Jamilla and Max have drawn bar models to solve this problem.

9,923 people live in a small town.

7,812 people are old enough to vote.

How many people are too young to vote?

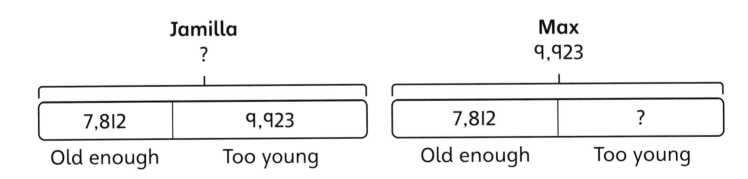

Discuss the bar models.

What is right and wrong about each one?

3 Write four different missing number problems that could be shown by this bar model.

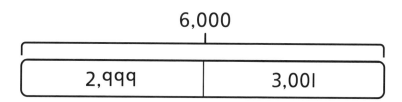

6,000

| 2,999 | 3,001 |

4 Draw your own bar models to show these calculations.

CHALLENGE

a) ☐ − 199 = 2,475

b) 2,475 − 199 = ☐

c) 199 = 2,475 − ☐

d) 199 + 2,475 = ☐

I don't think I need to draw four different bar models.

131

→ **Practice book 4A p94**

Problem solving – comparison

Discover

1 **a)** Show that Luis's score is more than Danny's using a bar model.

b) Calculate how much more Luis's score is than Danny's.

Share

I showed that Luis's score is more by drawing his bar wider.

a)

Luis

1,005	
899	?

Danny

A single bar model can be useful when you want to work out a whole or a part.

A comparison bar model is useful when you need to compare amounts.

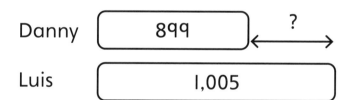

Danny [899] ⟵ ? ⟶

Luis [1,005]

b)

Th	H	T	O
⧸	⁹⧸0̸	⁹⧸0̸	¹5
−	8	9	9
	1	0	6

Th	H	T	O
⧸	¹0	0	6
−	9	0	0
	1	0	6

1,005 − 899 = 106. Luis has 106 more points than Danny.

Think together

1 Amelia is playing a game with her brother Jack.

Amelia has 1,050 points and Jack has 678 points.

How many more points does Amelia have?

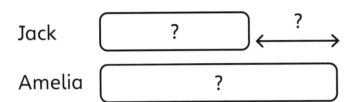

Jack   [?] ←?→

Amelia   [?]

	Th	H	T	O

2 Isla has 875 points more than her dad.

Her dad has 975 points.

Use the bar model to work out how many points Isla has.

[?] ←875→

[?]

This time I already know the difference. I wonder what I have to calculate here.

3 Choose whether to use a single bar model or a comparison bar model to show each of these problems. Then work out the answer to each problem.

a) I am thinking of a number. I subtract 100 from it and get 5,250. What was my number?

b) I am thinking of a number. Max thinks of a number 750 less than my number. His number is 5,250. What was my number?

c) I am thinking of a number. Then I add 750 to it. Now I have 5,250. What number did I think of to start with?

d) I am thinking of two numbers. One number is 2,000 more than the other. What could the numbers be?

I think one of these has more than one possible solution.

135

Problem solving – two steps

Discover

1 **a)** How far will Olivia need to run to complete the race?

b) Choose a way to check your calculation.

Share

I can think of two different ways to work out the answer.

a)

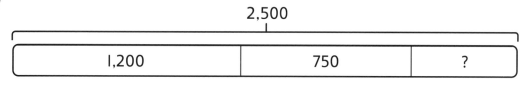

2,500

| 1,200 | 750 | ? |

Method 1
Subtract 1,200, then subtract 750.

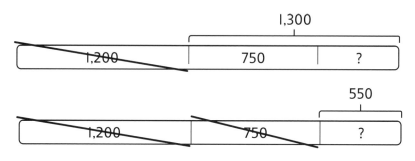

1,300

| 1,200 | 750 | ? |

550

| 1,200 | 750 | ? |

	Th	H	T	O
		2	5	0	0
−		1	2	0	0
		1	3	0	0

	Th	H	T	O
		X	¹²5̶ ¹	0	0
−			7	5	0
			5	5	0

Method 2
Add 1,200 and 750, and then subtract them from the whole.

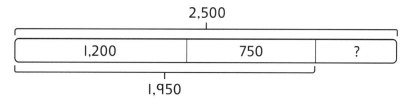

2,500

| 1,200 | 750 | ? |

1,950

	Th	H	T	O
	¹2̶	¹⁴5̶ ¹	0	0
−	1	9	5	0
		5	5	0

Olivia will need to run 550 m to complete the race.

b) Check by adding.

	Th	H	T	O
		1	2	0	0
+			7	5	0
		1	9	5	0

	Th	H	T	O
		1	9	5	0
+			5	5	0
		2	5	0	0
			1	1	

Think together

 a) Toshi, Amal and Jen ran in a relay race.

Jen ran 1,250 m, Amal ran 1,750 m and Toshi raced to the finish.

The race was 5,000 m long.

How far did Toshi run?

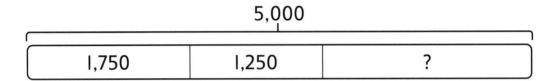

5,000		
1,750	1,250	?

I wonder which order I should do these steps in.

b) Toshi, Amal and Jen ran in another relay race.

How far did they run in total in this second race?

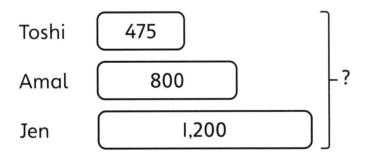

Toshi   475

Amal   800

Jen   1,200

?

You can show the whole at the side.

2 3,000 spectators attended the athletics event.

1,250 watched the running race.

300 more than that watched the javelin throwing.

The rest watched the long jump.

How many people watched the long jump?

I will draw a comparison model to show all the steps.

3 Alex and Emma ran 1,500 m in total.

Emma ran 1,000 m further than Alex.

How far did Alex run?

Draw a bar model and solve the problem.

CHALLENGE

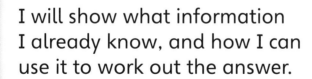

I will show what information I already know, and how I can use it to work out the answer.

139

→ Practice book 4A p100

Problem solving – multi-step problems

Discover

Base camp 0 m

Camp 1   2,450 m

Camp 2   5,275 m

Camp 3   7,299 m

Camp 4   8,158 m

Jen   Toshi   Amal

1 **a)** Jen has climbed 1,500 m higher than Camp 1.

She wants to know if she is now closer to Camp 1 or Camp 2.

How could she show the answer with a diagram?

b) Is Jen closer to Camp 1 or Camp 2?

Share

a)

I used a bar model to work out how far Jen is from Camp 2.

I used a different model to show the answer.

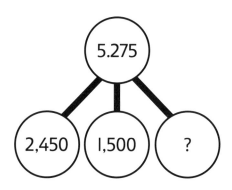

| 2,450 | 1,500 | ←—?—→ |

| 5,275 |

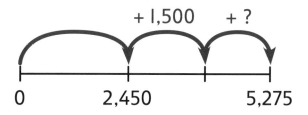

+ 1,500   + ?

0   2,450   5,275

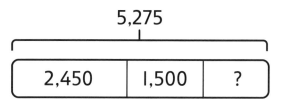

5,275

| 2,450 | 1,500 | ? |

All of the models show this problem. Choose one that helps you understand it.

b) To solve this problem, find out if the missing number is greater or less than 1,500.

This can be done in three steps:

1) 2,450 + 1,500 = 3,950

2) 5,275 − 3,950 = 1,325

3) 1,500 > 1,325, so Jen is closer to Camp 2.

Think together

① Amal climbed 1,245 m on Day 1, and then climbed 385 m less than that on Day 2.

He wants to work out how far he has climbed in total.

Decide which model shows this problem, and then solve it.

A
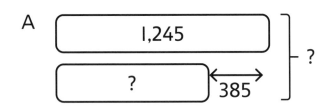

C

B
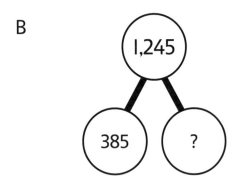

D
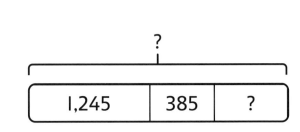

② The mountain is 6,895 m high.

After reaching the top, Jen climbed back down.

She climbed down 1,812 m on Day 1 and 1,259 m on Day 2.

After Day 3, she had 2,248 m left to climb.

Draw a diagram to show how far Jen climbed on Day 3, then calculate the answer.

I will try to work out if this is about parts and wholes, or comparing amounts.

142

3

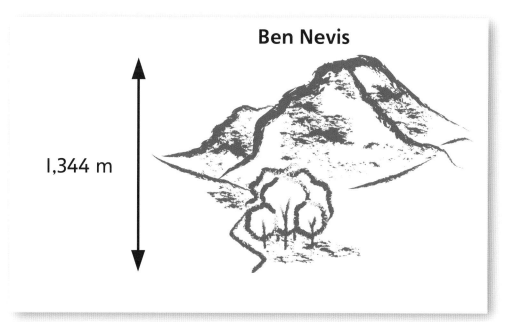

Ben Nevis

1,344 m

Ben Nevis is the tallest mountain in the UK.

Ben Nevis is 3,466 m shorter than Mont Blanc and Mont Blanc is 1,030 m taller than Mount Fuji.

Calculate the height of Mount Fuji.

Use a model to show the problem.

This problem has two steps, so I will draw two different models.

We are comparing three mountains. I wonder if I can draw three bars in one model.

143

End of unit check

1 Which column method completes this addition?

Th	H	T	O
1,000 1,000 1,000		10	1 1 1 1 1
1,000 1,000	100 100	10	1

A

Th	H	T	O
3	1	0	5
+ 2	2	1	1
5	3	1	6

B

Th	H	T	O
²3̸	¹0	1	5
− 2	2	1	1
	8	0	4

C

Th	H	T	O
3	0	1	5
+ 2	2	1	1
5	2	2	6

D

Th	H	T	O
3	0	1	5
+ 2	2	1	1
5	0	2	6

2 Which subtraction requires only one exchange?

A

Th	H	T	O
4	1	2	3
− 1	9	9	8

B

Th	H	T	O
4	9	9	8
− 1	2	3	4

C

Th	H	T	O
4	3	8	2
− 1	2	8	9

D

Th	H	T	O
4	9	1	8
− 1	2	3	4

3 Which calculation gives the same answer as 5,000 − 997?

A 5,001 − 996

B 4,999 − 996

C 4,999 − 998

D 5,001 − 999

4 Which calculation does not check 6,025 − 1,834 = 4,191?

A 6,025 − 4,191   **C** 1,834 + 4,191

B 4,191 − 1,834   **D** 4,191 + 1,834

5 Bella scored 1,250 points and Ebo scored 425 points.

Which bar model shows the difference between Bella's score and Ebo's score?

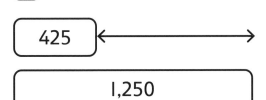

A

| 425 | ⟵⟶ |

| 1,250 |

C

| ? |
| 425 | 1,250 |

B

| 425 | 1,250 |

D

| 1,250 |
| | ⟵⟶ 425 |

6 Sofia paid £2,500 for a holiday.

Amal paid £1,200 less than Sofia for a holiday.

How much did they pay altogether?

145

→ Practice book 4A p106

Unit 4
Measure – area

In this unit we will …

⚡ Learn what 'area' means

⚡ Find areas of shapes by counting squares

⚡ Draw shapes with different areas

⚡ Compare the areas of different shapes

How many small squares fit into this large square?

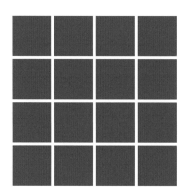

We will need some maths words. Which of these are new?

| space | area | rectangle |

| square | rectilinear shape | unit |

| larger | greater | smaller |

Which shape do you think is larger? Why?

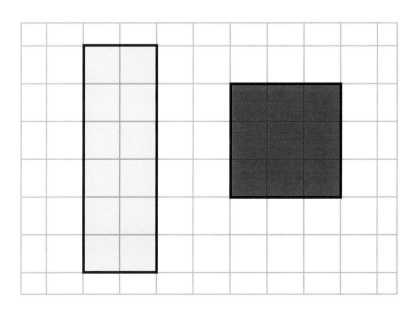

What is area?

Discover

1 **a)** Which mat has more **space** for the cats?

b) Use counters to fill up each mat.

Share

The **area** of a shape is the name we give to the space it takes up.

The larger the shape, the larger its area.

a)

There is less space for the cats. This mat has a smaller area.

There is more space for the cats. This mat has a larger area.

b) Another way to find the answer is to use different objects to measure area.

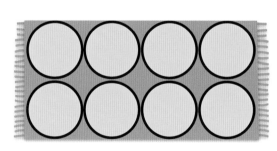 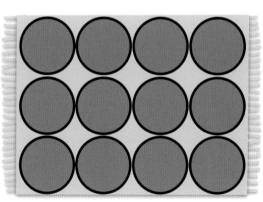

Using counters is a good way to measure area.

149

Think together

1 How many counters can you fit inside this rectangle?

I predict I can fit 10 counters in the rectangle.

The area of the rectangle is ☐ counters.

2 How many counters can you fit inside this circle?

The area of the circle is ☐ counters.

CHALLENGE

3 Here are two rectangles.

A

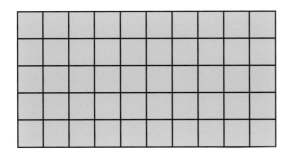

B

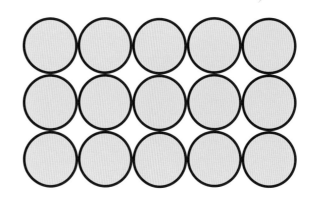

50 plastic squares

15 counters

Rectangle A is larger because 50 is more than 15.

I am not sure that is right.

Why does Astrid need to think again?

→ **Practice book 4A p109**

Measure area using squares

Discover

Luis

Lexi

Shape A

Shape B

1 **a)** What is the area of each shape?

b) Draw or make your own shape on a grid like these.

Share

a) The **units** we can use to measure area are squares.

Count the squares to find which shape is larger.

I drew lines to divide the shapes into squares. Then I wrote numbers inside to help me count them.

I wonder if it would help to place a counter on each square and then count them.

b) Count the squares to measure the area of your shape.

Here are two examples of shapes.

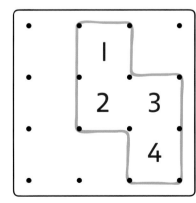
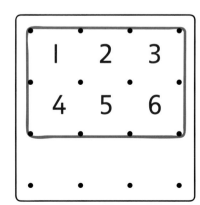

Think together

1 Count the squares in each shape to find the area.

Shape A Shape B Shape C

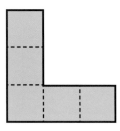 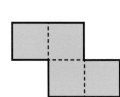 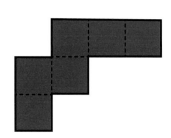

The area of shape A is ☐ squares.

The area of shape B is ☐ squares.

The area of shape C is ☐ squares.

2 What is the area of these shapes?

A B C

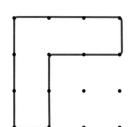

Shape	Area
A	
B	
C	

3 Ash has covered these rectangles with small paper squares.

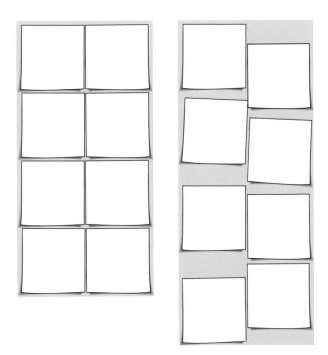

These rectangles both have an area of 8 squares. They are the same size.

I do not think this is right. Don't worry, you can learn from your mistake!

What has Ash done wrong?

Explain why you think that this will give the wrong answer.

155

Count squares

Discover

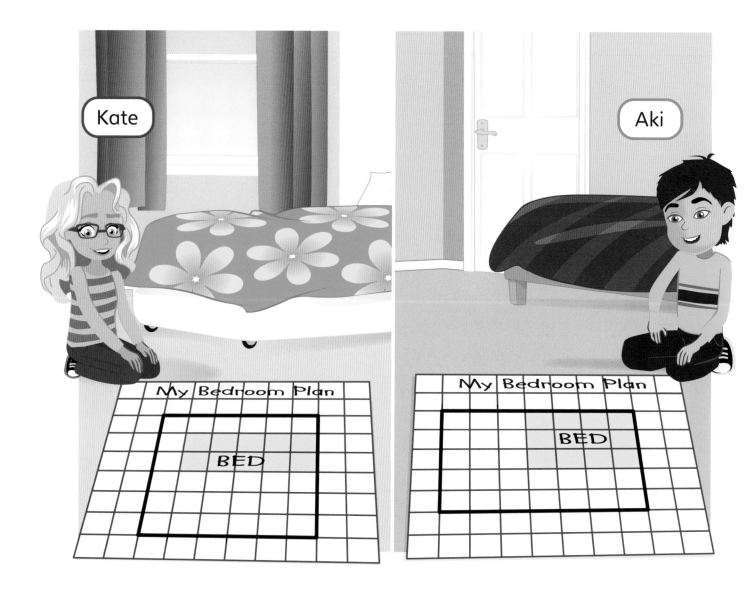

1 **a)** What is the area of each bed?

b) What is the area of empty space Kate and Aki each have in their bedroom?

Share

a) We can use squared paper to help find the area of different shapes.

I numbered each square to make sure I did not miss any.

I thought of a way to use times-table facts to help.

1	2	3	4	5
6	7	8	9	10

1	2	3	4	5

Kate's bed has 2 rows of 5 squares.

$2 \times 5 = 10$

1	2	3	4
5	6	7	8
9	10	11	12

1	2	3	4

Aki's bed has 3 rows of 4 squares.

$3 \times 4 = 12$

b) Count the squares to find the area of the empty space.

1	2	3	4	5	6
7					
8					
9	10	11	12	13	14
15	16	17	18	19	20
21	22	23	24	25	26

1	2	3				
4	5	6				
7	8	9				
10	11	12	13	14	15	16
17	18	19	20	21	22	23

Kate has **26** squares of empty space in her bedroom.

Aki has **23** squares of empty space in his bedroom.

Think together

1 Find the areas of these three rectangles by counting the squares.

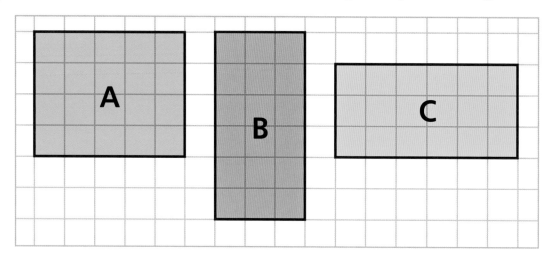

A = ☐ squares   B = ☐ squares   C = ☐ squares

2 Work out the areas of these two rectilinear shapes.

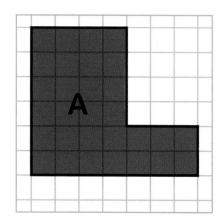

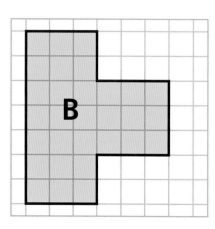

A rectilinear shape is a shape with straight sides that always meet at right angles. Squares and rectangles are rectilinear shapes.

A = ☐ squares   B = ☐ squares

3 Part of the rectangle has been hidden.

What is the area of the rectangle?

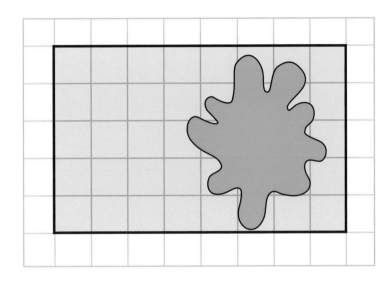

I can count all the squares I can see.

I'm going to calculate all of the squares in the shape.

The area of this shape is ⬜ squares.

→ **Practice book 4A p115**

Make shapes

Discover

1 **a)** Join 4 square slabs to make a rectilinear shape.

b) Join 5 square slabs to make a rectilinear shape.

Share

a) When squares are used to make a rectilinear shape, they should touch at the side, not just the corner.

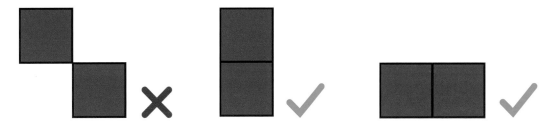

To show the shapes with an area of 4 paving slabs, we can use 4 squares. They can be arranged in the following different ways.

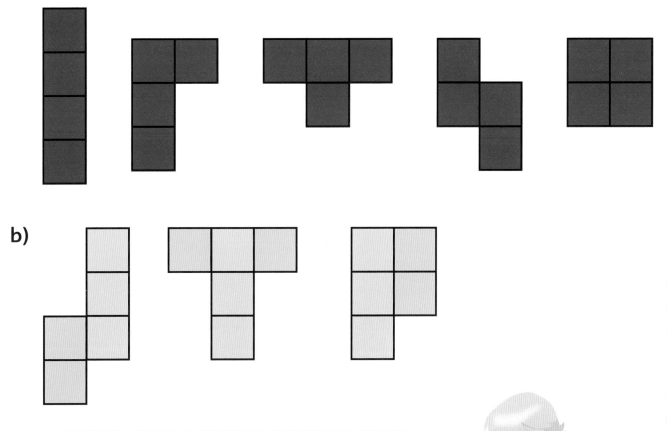

b)

I found 3 shapes with an area of 5. I wonder if there are more?

Think together

1 Holly has drawn a shape with 8 squares.

Draw your own shape on squared paper.

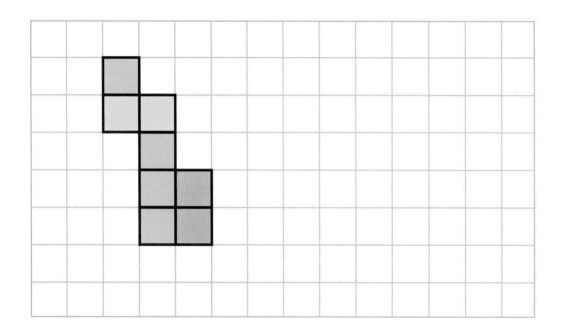

2 Draw a square with an area of 25.

Draw a rectangle with an area of 24.

How many solutions can you find?

I will try to be systematic.

3 Holly has 8 squares.

She wants to make a rectilinear shape using all her squares.

Which of these shapes can she make?

A   B   C   D

Hmmm … I think there is only one possible shape here.

You may be right, but how do you know?

163

→ Practice book 4A p118

Compare area

Discover

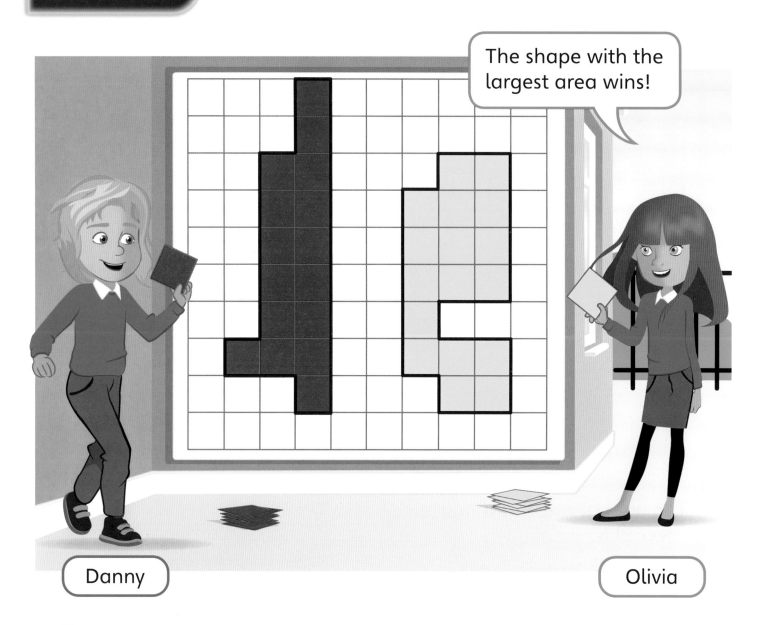

The shape with the largest area wins!

Danny

Olivia

1 **a)** Who is winning the game? How do you know?

b) Which is larger: the area of the board that is covered or the area of the board that is not covered?

Share

a) The more squares that fit inside a shape, the larger its area.

Danny

Olivia

Count the squares inside each shape.

Danny's red shape has an area of 16 squares.

Olivia's yellow shape has an area of 17 squares.

17 > 16, so Olivia is winning the game.

b) The total area of the board is:

10 × 10 = 100 squares.

1	2	3	4	5	6	7	8	9	10
2									
3									
4									
5									
6									
7									
8									
9									
10									

The area of the board that is covered is:

16 + 17 = 33 squares.

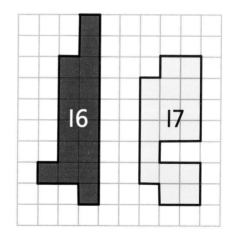

100 − 33 = 67

33 < 67

The area of the board that is not covered is larger.

Think together

1 Which shape has the larger area?

Predict which shape you think first, then check.

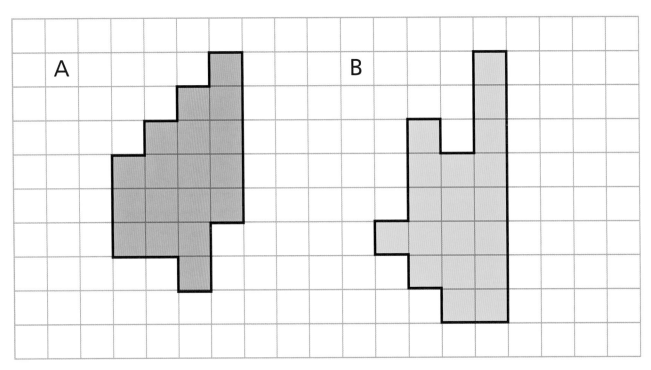

2 a) Find the area of each of these letters.

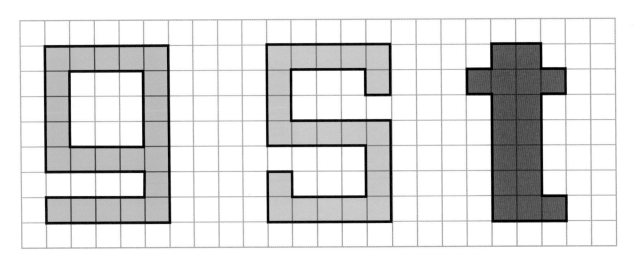

b) Put the letters in order of size, from smallest to largest area.

3 The shape with the **greater** area wins. Who has won the game and why?

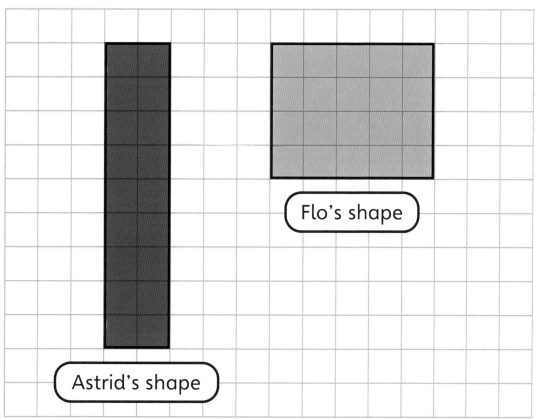

Flo's shape

Astrid's shape

I win! My purple shape is a lot taller than your rectangle, so the area must be greater.

I think we need to do something else to be able to compare areas.

167

→ Practice book 4A p121

End of unit check

1 What is the area of a shape?

  A Area is the distance all the way around a shape.

  B Area is the length of a shape.

  C Area is the space inside a shape.

  D Area is the width of a shape.

2 What is the area of the rectangle?

  A 18 squares

  B 7 squares

  C 12 squares

  D 14 squares

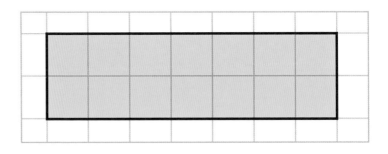

3 One of the shapes below does not have an area of 36 squares. Which is it?

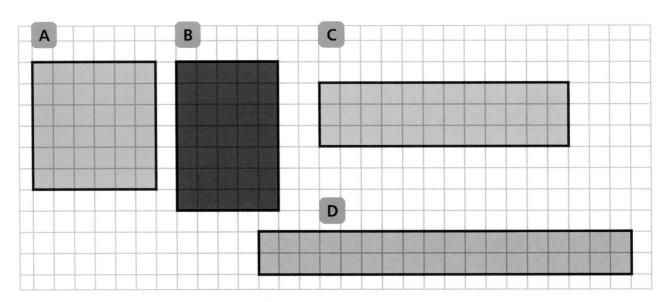

4 Which shape has the largest area?

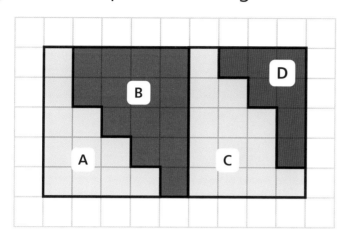

5 Which of these shapes is it not possible to make using 9 squares?

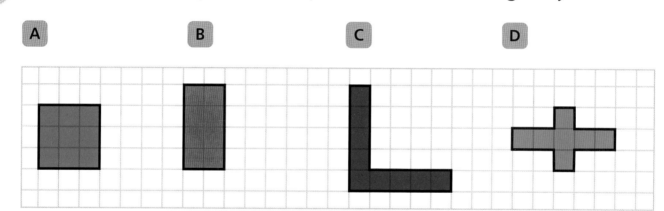

A B C D

6 What is the area of the shaded shape?

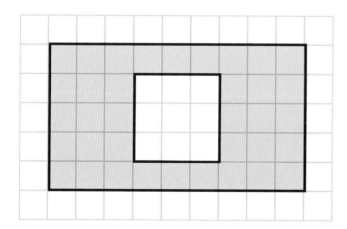

The area of the shaded shape is ▢ squares.

→ Practice book 4A p124

Unit 5
Multiplication and division ❶

In this unit we will ...

⚡ Multiply and divide by 0 and 1

⚡ Learn all of our times-tables from 1 to 12

⚡ Understand related multiplication and division facts

⚡ Multiply three numbers

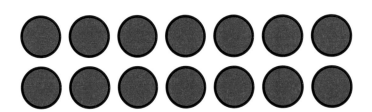

Do you remember what this is called? Use it to find 2 × 7 or 7 × 2.

We will need some maths words. Are any of these new?

multiply (×) divide (÷)

multiplication fact division fact

factor groups of times-table array

product fact family related fact

We need to use the number line too!
Use it to support your counting in groups.

$$6 × 9 = 54$$

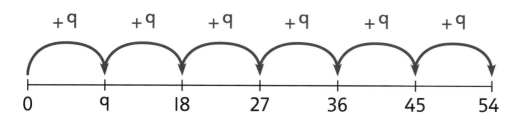

Multiples of 3

Discover

1 **a)** Use 12 counters.

Make **groups of** 3.

Make 3 equal groups.

b) Write multiplication and division facts for each arrangement.

Share

a) 12 is a multiple of 3.

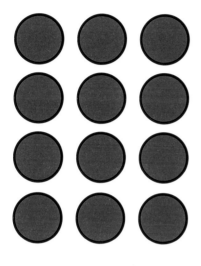

12 is 4 groups of 3.

12 is 3 groups of 4

b)

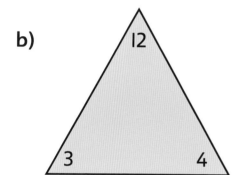

$3 \times 4 = 12$
$4 \times 3 = 12$

$12 \div 3 = 4$
$12 \div 4 = 3$

This triangle shows the **product** 12 and the **factors** 3 and 4.

173

Think together

1 Count in multiples of 3.

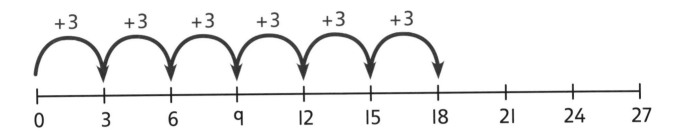

2 Use the array to complete the triangle.

Write 2 multiplication facts and 2 division facts that match the array and the triangle.

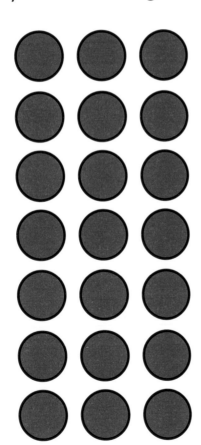

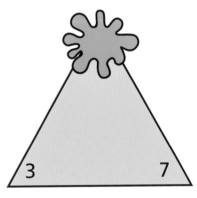

$$\square \times \square = \square$$

$$\square \times \square = \square$$

$$\square \div \square = \square$$

$$\square \div \square = \square$$

3 **a)** Use the cubes to make towers of 3.

I will use all cubes.

I wonder if that is possible.

b) Which of these numbers are **not** multiples of 3?

9, 13, 23, 30

175

Multiply and divide by 6

Discover

1   a) Toshi has 7 full egg boxes.

   How many eggs are there in total inside these boxes?

   b) Under the table is a tray of 30 eggs.

   How many egg boxes can be filled using the eggs in the tray?

Share

a) There are 7 full egg boxes. Each box holds 6 eggs.

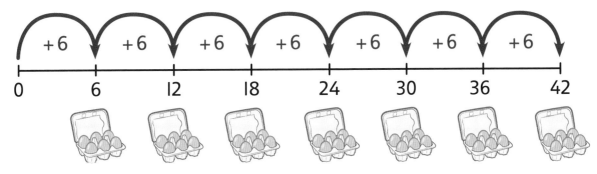

6 + 6 + 6 + 6 + 6 + 6 + 6 = 42

7 × 6 = 42

There are 42 eggs in the boxes.

I counted on in 6s.

b) There are 30 eggs in the tray. Each egg box can hold 6 eggs.

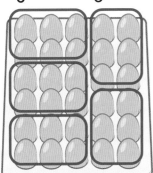

I counted back in 6s to divide.

30 ÷ 6 = 5

The eggs in the tray will fill 5 egg boxes.

Think together

1   How many eggs are there in total?

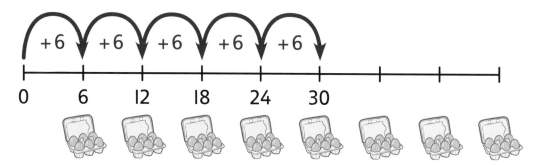

☐ + ☐ + ☐ + ☐ + ☐ + ☐ + ☐ + ☐ = ☐

or

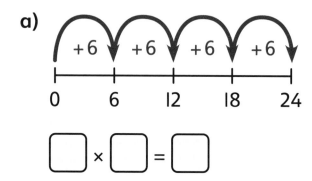

☐ × ☐ = ☐   There are ☐ eggs in total.

2   What calculations are shown on the number lines?

a)

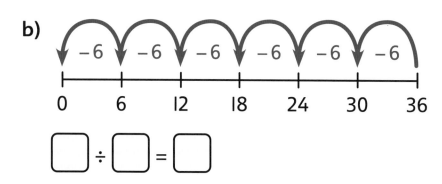

☐ × ☐ = ☐

b)

☐ ÷ ☐ = ☐

a) A supermarket displays apples in baskets of 18.

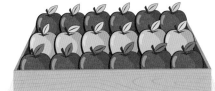

I will make an array using counters.

How many apples are there in total?

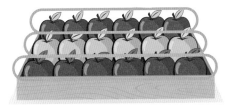

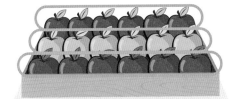

I wonder if I can multiply by 6 to find the total number of apples? I've grouped the apples to help me.

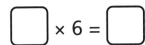 × 6 = ☐

b) How many apples would there be in 4 boxes?

179

→ Practice book 4A p129

6 times-table and division facts

Discover

$$0 \times 6 = 0$$
$$1 \times 6 = 6$$
$$2 \times 6 = 12$$
$$3 \times 6 = 18$$
$$4 \times 6 = 24$$
$$5 \times 6 = 30$$
$$6 \times 6 =$$
$$7 \times 6 =$$
$$8 \times 6 =$$
$$9 \times 6 =$$
$$10 \times 6 =$$
$$11 \times 6 =$$
$$12 \times 6 =$$

$$42 \div 6 = ?$$

1 a) Complete the 6 times-table.

 b) Use the times-table to complete the division fact.

Share

a)

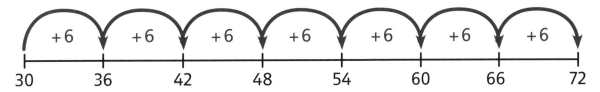

I counted on in 6s from 30.

+6 +6 +6 +6 +6 +6 +6

30   36   42   48   54   60   66   72

The missing answers are:

0 × 6 = 0
1 × 6 = 6
2 × 6 = 12
3 × 6 = 18
4 × 6 = 24
5 × 6 = 30
6 × 6 = 36
7 × 6 = 42
8 × 6 = 48
9 × 6 = 54
10 × 6 = 60
11 × 6 = 66
12 × 6 = 72

If I know my 6 times-table, I can do division facts.

b)

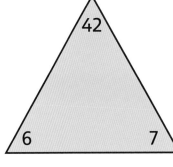

42

6   7

42 ÷ 6 = 7

This fact shows me:

7 × 6 = 42
6 × 7 = 42
42 ÷ 6 = 7
42 ÷ 7 = 6

181

Think together

1 Use the 6 times-table to find the total number of pencils.

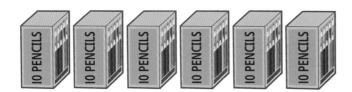

Is that 10 groups of 6 or 6 groups of 10? Does it matter?

2 Write two multiplication and two division facts for each array.

a)

☐ × ☐ = ☐

☐ × ☐ = ☐

☐ ÷ ☐ = ☐

☐ ÷ ☐ = ☐

b)

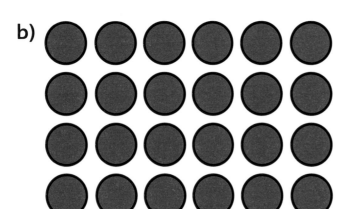

☐ × ☐ = ☐

☐ × ☐ = ☐

☐ ÷ ☐ = ☐

☐ ÷ ☐ = ☐

3 **a)** Work out 3 × 5.

Now work out 3 × 6.

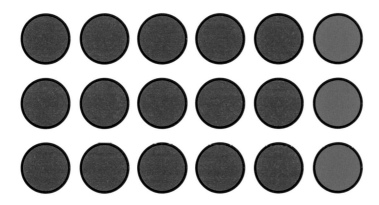

How does the array show that 6 × 3 = 5 × 3 + 3?

b) How can you use the 5 times-table to work out the 6 times-table?

I think I need to add something to each number in the 5 times-table. It seems different each time.

183

→ Practice book 4A p132

Multiply and divide by 9

Discover

1 a) Reena has a puzzle cube.

How many faces are on the cube?

How many squares are on each face?

b) Calculate the total number of squares on the whole cube.

Share

a) A cube has 6 faces.

There are 9 squares on each face.

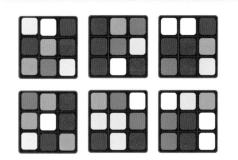

b)

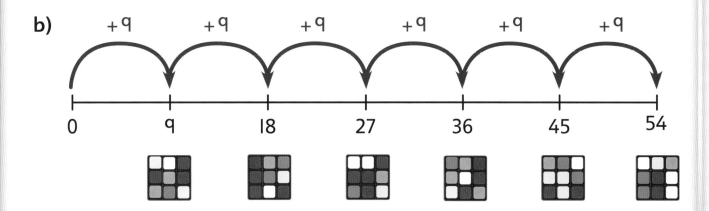

$9 + 9 + 9 + 9 + 9 + 9 = 54$

$6 \times 9 = 54$

There are 54 coloured squares in total.

I counted in 9s.

I used my 6
times-table
to check.

185

Think together

1 Count in multiples of 9.

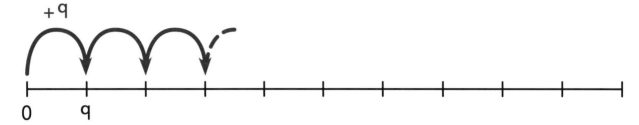

2 a)

27 TOY PEOPLE £ 9.00   27 TOY PEOPLE £ 9.00   27 TOY PEOPLE £ 9.00   27 TOY PEOPLE £ 9.00   27 TOY PEOPLE £ 9.00

Aki buys 5 boxes.

How much does he spend?

Aki spends £ ☐.

b) Ambika has £27.

How many boxes can she buy?

Ambika can buy ☐ boxes.

I will use a number line to help me.

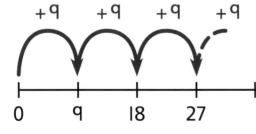

3 **a)** Work out 3 × 10.

Now work out 3 × 9.

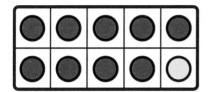 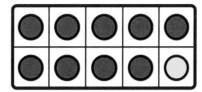 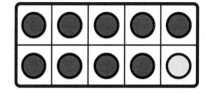

b) Complete these multiplications.

5 × 10 = ☐   5 × 9 = ☐

7 × 10 = ☐   7 × 9 = ☐

c) What do you notice?

4

39   144   279   521   522   752

CHALLENGE

a) Which of these numbers can be divided by 9?

b) Find three 3-digit numbers that can be divided by 9.

To test if a number divides by 9:
• add up the digits of the number
• if this total divides by 9 then the original number also divides by 9.

187

→ Practice book 4A p135

9 times-table and division facts

Discover

1 **a)** Between them, how many turns have Bella and Danny had so far?

b) If Bella and Danny have had 63 turns between them, how many games have they played?

Share

a) Each game has 9 turns. There are 4 games.

$4 \times 9 = 36$

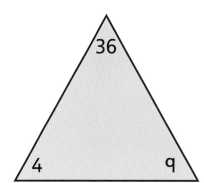

There are four facts:

$4 \times 9 = 36$ $36 \div 9 = 4$

$9 \times 4 = 36$ $36 \div 4 = 9$

Between them, they have had 36 turns so far.

b)

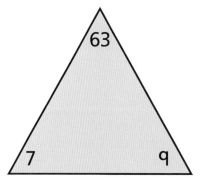

They have played 7 games.

$63 \div 9 = 7$

Think together

1 Complete the multiplication and division facts.

a)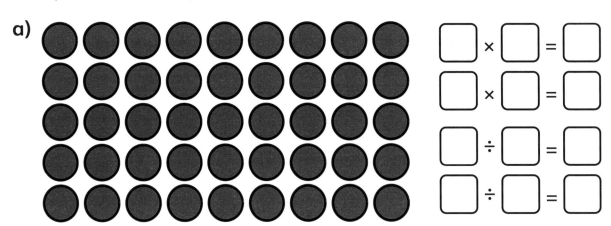

$$\boxed{} \times \boxed{} = \boxed{}$$

$$\boxed{} \times \boxed{} = \boxed{}$$

$$\boxed{} \div \boxed{} = \boxed{}$$

$$\boxed{} \div \boxed{} = \boxed{}$$

2 Complete the multiplication and division facts.

a) $0 \times 0 = \boxed{}$

b) $11 \times 9 = \boxed{}$

c) $63 \div 9 = \boxed{}$

d) $1 \times 9 = \boxed{}$

e) $12 \times 9 = \boxed{}$

f) $54 \div 9 = \boxed{}$

g) $5 \times 9 = \boxed{}$

h) $36 \div 9 = \boxed{}$

i) $8 \times 9 = \boxed{}$

j) $18 \div 9 = \boxed{}$

I will use ten frames to help me work out the answers I don't know.

3 **a)** Work out the hidden numbers.

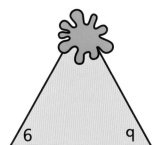  

6 9   7 9   8 9

CHALLENGE

I always forget this fact.
I need a way to remember it.

You can multiply by
10 and then subtract
the number you
were multiplying.

So to multiply 5 by 9,
multiply 5 by 10 first
and then subtract 5.

b) Use Sparks' method to work out the following.

1 × 9	5 × 9	9 × 9
2 × 9	6 × 9	10 × 9
3 × 9	7 × 9	11 × 9
4 × 9	8 × 9	12 × 9

191

→ Practice book 4A p138

The 3, 6 and 9 times-tables

Discover

Multiples of 3

Multiples of 6

1 **a)** Place the number cards in the correct place in the sorting circles.

   b) Can you think of a number that would just go in the Multiples of 6 circle?

Share

a)

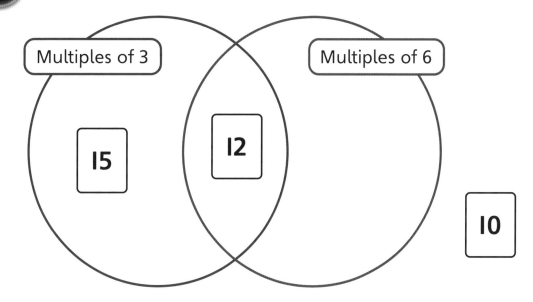

15 is a multiple of 3 but not of 6.

12 is a multiple of both 3 and 6.

10 is not a multiple of 3 or 6.

b)   The large section of the Multiples of 6 circle remains empty.

All multiples of 6 are also multiples of 3.

$1 \times 3 = 3$

$2 \times 3 = 6 \longrightarrow 1 \times 6 = 6$

$3 \times 3 = 9$

$4 \times 3 = 12 \longrightarrow 2 \times 6 = 12$

$5 \times 3 = 15$

$6 \times 3 = 18 \longrightarrow 3 \times 6 = 18$

No numbers will only go in the Multiples of 6 circle.

Think together

1 Use 3 different-coloured counters.

1	2	3	4	5	6	7	8	9	10
11	12	13	14	15	16	17	18	19	20
21	22	23	24	25	26	27	28	29	30
31	32	33	34	35	36	37	38	39	40
41	42	43	44	45	46	47	48	49	50
51	52	53	54	55	56	57	58	59	60
61	62	63	64	65	66	67	68	69	70
71	72	73	74	75	76	77	78	79	80
81	82	83	84	85	86	87	88	89	90
91	92	93	94	95	96	97	98	99	100

Use one colour to cover multiples of 3.

Use another colour to cover multiples of 6.

Use the third colour to cover multiples of 9.

What do you notice?

2 Are these statements always, sometimes or never true?

A multiple of 3 is odd.

A multiple of 6 is a multiple of 9.

A multiple of 3 is a multiple of 6.

How do you know?

3 **a)**

2 × 2							
3 × 2	3 × 3						
4 × 2	4 × 3	4 × 4					
5 × 2	5 × 3	5 × 4	5 × 5				
6 × 2	6 × 3	6 × 4	6 × 5	6 × 6			
7 × 2	7 × 3	7 × 4	7 × 5	7 × 6	7 × 7		
8 × 2	8 × 3	8 × 4	8 × 5	8 × 6	8 × 7	8 × 8	
9 × 2	9 × 3	9 × 4	9 × 5	9 × 6	9 × 7	9 × 8	9 × 9

Find all the multiples of 3.

Find all the multiples of 6.

Find all the multiples of 9.

b) Sort the facts into three lists.

I know for certain.

I might know.

I don't know yet.

I will use this grid to
learn with a partner.
We can test each other.

195

→ **Practice book 4A p141**

Multiply and divide by 7

Discover

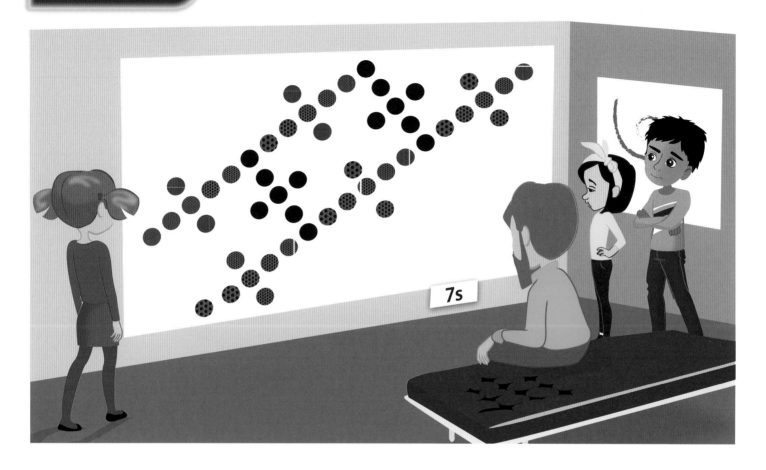

1 **a)** Why do you think the painting is called '7s'?

How many groups of 7 are there?

How many circles are there in total?

b) Another picture is made using groups of 7 circles.

There are 28 circles.

How many groups of 7 circles are there?

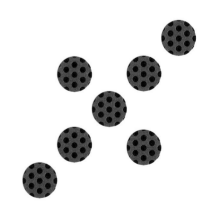

Share

a) The picture is made up of groups of 7 circles.

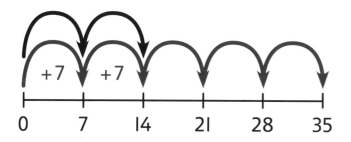

$5 \times 7 = 35$

There are 35 dotted circles.

$2 \times 7 = 14$

There are 14 black circles.

$7 \times 7 = 49$

There are 49 circles in total.

I worked out how many patterned circles and how many black circles there are. Then I found the total.

b)

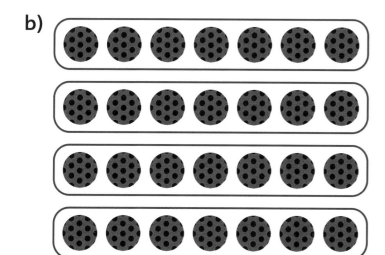

To group the circles I made an array.

$28 \div 7 = 4$

There are 4 groups of 7 circles.

Think together

1 Count in multiples of 7.

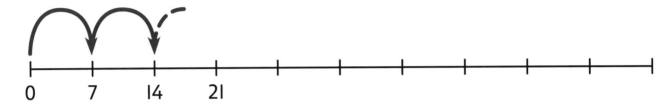

0   7   14   21

2 a)

HATS £7.00 each

Alex buys 6 hats.

How much money does she spend?

b)

HATS £7.00 each

Zac has £56.

How many hats can he buy?

Use the number line to help you.

3

I wonder which is longer, 40 days or 6 weeks?

Are there more or fewer than 4 weeks in September?

Lexi

Mr Jones

Remember, September has 30 days.

Explain how to help Lexi and Mr Jones answer their questions.

To compare 40 days and 6 weeks I could do a division or a multiplication.

I know there are 7 days in a week.

199

→ **Practice book 4A p144**

7 times-table and division facts

Discover

1 **a)** Which treasure chest does each key open?
Explain why.

b) What keys would open the other chests?

Share

a) The treasure chests that are opened by the keys are the answers to the multiplications.

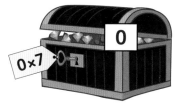  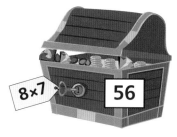

$0 \times 7 = 0$

The 0 × 7 key opens the 0 chest.

$4 \times 7 = 28$

The 4 × 7 key opens the 28 chest.

$8 \times 7 = 56$

The 8 × 7 key opens the 56 chest.

b)

$77 \div 7 = 11$

11×7

7

$7 \div 7 = 1$

1×7

$42 \div 7 = 6$

6×7

$14 \div 7 = 2$

2×7

$70 \div 7 = 10$

10×7

$63 \div 7 = 9$

9×7

Think together

1 There are 7 counters in each stack.

Use multiplication facts to work out how many counters there are in total.

☐ × 7 = ☐

7 × ☐ = ☐

2 Complete the multiplication and division facts.

a) 5 × 7 = 35

7 × 5 = ☐

35 ÷ 7 = ☐

35 ÷ 5 = ☐

b) 12 × 7 = ☐

☐ × ☐ = ☐

☐ ÷ ☐ = ☐

☐ ÷ ☐ = ☐

You might want to make an array to help you.

3 **a)** Help Danny to work out the multiplications.

Danny: I haven't learnt my 7 times-table yet.

Jamie: But you already know the 2 and 5 times-tables.

3 × 5 = ☐

3 × 2 = ☐

3 × 7 = ☐

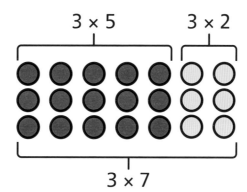

3 × 5   3 × 2

3 × 7

b) Use the facts you already know to complete the 7 times-table.

1 × 7	5 × 7	9 × 7
2 × 7	6 × 7	10 × 7
3 × 7	7 × 7	11 × 7
4 × 7	8 × 7	12 × 7

I will create arrays using the 5 and 2 times-tables to work out the answers.

203

11 and 12 times-tables and division facts

Discover

Alex

Max

1 **a)** Which 11 times-table fact has Max made?

Which times-table fact has Alex made?

b) Count in multiples of 11.

Then count in multiples of 12.

Share

a) Max made this fact from the 11 times-table.

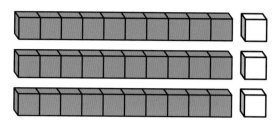

$$3 \times 11 = 33$$

Alex made this fact.

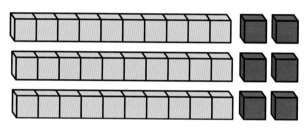

$$3 \times 12 = 36$$

I noticed that 0 and 132 appear in both the 11 and the 12 times-tables.

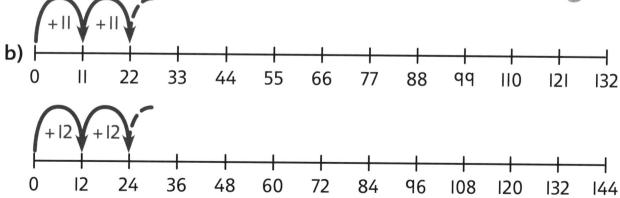

b)

Think together

1. Use cubes to work out 7 × 11.

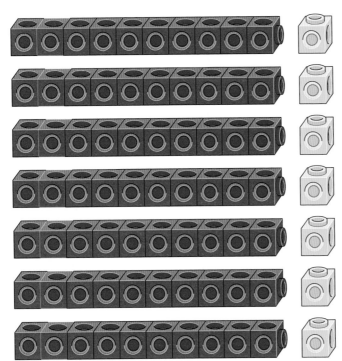

$7 \times 11 = \boxed{}$

2. What times-table facts are shown here?

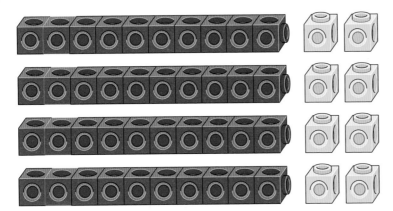

$\boxed{} \times \boxed{} = \boxed{}$

$\boxed{} \times \boxed{} = \boxed{}$

I think I have seen some of these facts before in other times-tables, but where?

3 Olivia uses base 10 equipment to show 7 × 12.

I've noticed that in each row I have a line of 10 cubes and 2 extra cubes. Perhaps I can use these times-tables to find the solution.

Olivia

a) Explain how Olivia can use number facts from the 10 and 2 times-tables to get the correct answer.

b) Complete these calculations.

| 4 × 12 | 9 × 12 | 60 ÷ 12 |

| 11 × 12 | 84 ÷ 12 | 144 ÷ 12 |

I think there is more than one way to find the solutions to these multiplications.

207

Multiply by 1 and 0

Discover

1 **a)** How many jam tarts does each child have?

Write a multiplication calculation for each one.

b) What mistakes have Mo and Emma made?

Share

a) Each child has a number of plates on which their jam tarts are grouped.

I worked out how many groups and how many in each group.

There are 3 groups of 2.

$3 \times 2 = 6$

Jamilla has 6 tarts.

There are 3 groups of 1.

$3 \times 1 = 3$

Mo has 3 tarts.

There are 3 groups of 0.

$3 \times 0 = 0$

Emma has 0 tarts.

b) Mo said, '$3 \times 1 = 4$.'

Mo added instead of multiplying.

$3 \times 1 = 3$

Emma said, '$3 \times 0 = 3$.'

Emma thinks that multiplying by 0 is the same as multiplying by 1.

$3 \times 0 = 0$

Emma has made a common mistake. Any number multiplied by 0 is always 0.

209

Think together

1 How many apples are there in total?

a)

b)

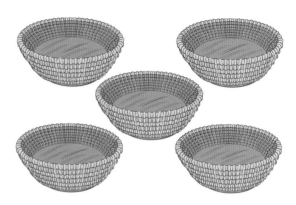

☐ × ☐ = ☐   ☐ × ☐ = ☐

2 Put counters in the boxes to represent each calculation.

 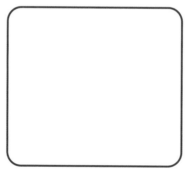 

a) 3 × 4 = 12   **c)** 3 × 0 = 0

b) 3 × 1 = 3   **d)** 2 × 3 = 6

Unit 5: Multiplication and division (1), Lesson 10

3 Mo and Emma are investigating multiplying by 1 and 0.

a) Mo is investigating what happens when you multiply by 1.

Help Mo to work out the missing numbers.

$5 \times 1 = \boxed{}$ $\boxed{} = 6 \times 1$ $\boxed{} = 10 \times 1$

$1 \times 15 = \boxed{}$ $\boxed{} \times 1 = 17$ $1 \times \boxed{} = 183$

What do you think Mo notices?

> To help me multiply by 1, I will make an array.

b) Emma is investigating what happens when you multiply by 0.

Help Emma to work out the missing numbers.

$5 \times 0 = \boxed{}$ $6 \times 0 = \boxed{}$ $\boxed{} = 10 \times 0$

$0 \times 15 = \boxed{}$ $17 \times \boxed{} = 0$ $\boxed{} \times 183 = 0$

What do you think Emma notices?

> I think there are similarities in each of Emma's answers.

211

→ Practice book 4A p153

Divide by 1 and itself

Discover

1 **a)** How many bags of hay does Ted have?

How many bags of hay do Rose and Baz have?

What division could you use to work out how much hay each horse gets?

b) Write a division to share the hay between Jo's horses.

Share

> I will share out the bags of hay one at a time.

a)

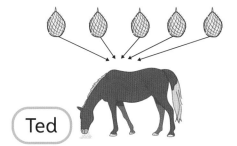

Ted

Baz

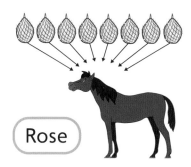

Rose

There are 5 bags of hay.

There is 1 horse.

$5 \div 1 = 5$

The horse will get 5 bags of hay.

There are 3 bags of hay.

There is 1 horse.

$3 \div 1 = 3$

The horse will get 3 bags of hay.

There are 8 bags of hay.

There is 1 horse.

$8 \div 1 = 8$

The horse will get 8 bags of hay.

b)

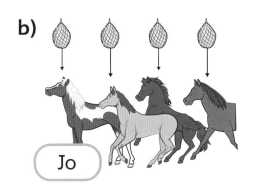

Jo

> When you divide a number by itself the answer is always 1.

There are 4 bags of hay.

There are 4 horses.

$4 \div 4 = 1$

Each horse will get 1 bag of hay.

213

Think together

1 Complete the fact family.

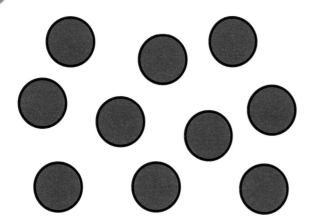

$10 \times 1 = \boxed{}$ $10 \div 1 = \boxed{}$

$1 \times 10 = \boxed{}$ $10 \div 10 = \boxed{}$

2 Complete the fact family for the arrays.

a)

$\boxed{} \times \boxed{} = \boxed{}$

$\boxed{} \times \boxed{} = \boxed{}$

$\boxed{} \div \boxed{} = \boxed{}$

$\boxed{} \div \boxed{} = \boxed{}$

b)

$\boxed{} \times \boxed{} = \boxed{}$

$\boxed{} \times \boxed{} = \boxed{}$

$\boxed{} \div \boxed{} = \boxed{}$

$\boxed{} \div \boxed{} = \boxed{}$

3 Here are some division calculations.

Set A	Set B
4 ÷ 1	4 ÷ 4
5 ÷ 1	5 ÷ 5
7 ÷ 1	7 ÷ 7
10 ÷ 1	10 ÷ 10
15 ÷ 1	15 ÷ 15
32 ÷ 1	32 ÷ 32
142 ÷ 1	142 ÷ 142

I've noticed that some of the answers are the same.

a) What are the answers to the divisions?

b) What patterns or rules do you notice?

Try making up your own divisions that have an answer of 1. What do you notice?

215

Multiply three numbers

Discover

1 **a)** Write a multiplication for the stickers on 1 sheet.

b) In total, how many stickers are there on the teacher's desk?

Share

a) There are 5 rows of 2 stickers.

$2 + 2 + 2 + 2 + 2 = 10$

Or, $5 × 2 = 10$

There are 10 stickers on 1 sheet.

b)

$5 × 2 × 3 = 30$

$10 \quad × 3 = 30$

I worked out how many stickers there are on each sheet and multiplied by 3.

$5 × 2 × 3 = 30$

$5 × \quad 6 \quad = 30$

I first counted how many are in each row. There are 5 rows. The answer is the same!

There are 30 stickers, in total, on the teacher's desk.

Think together

1 Complete the two methods to work out how many stickers there are on 6 sheets.

5×2 $\times 6 =$ ☐   or 2×5 $\times 6 =$ ☐

☐ $\times 6 =$ ☐   ☐ $\times 6 =$ ☐

There are ☐ stickers on 6 sheets.

2 A box contains 3 rows of 6 doughnuts.

a) How many doughnuts are there in 2 boxes?

☐ × ☐ × ☐ = ☐

There are ☐ doughnuts in 2 boxes.

b) How many doughnuts are there in 5 boxes?

There are ☐ doughnuts in 5 boxes.

You could draw a diagram to help you.

3 **a)** Luis and Isla are working out the answer to this calculation.

$$9 \times 2 \times 5$$

I did $9 \times 2 = 18$ and then $18 \times 5 = 90$.

I did $2 \times 5 = 10$ and then multiplied my answer by 9. $10 \times 9 = 90$

Luis

Isla

Which method do you think is more efficient? Why?

b) What is the most efficient method to use to work out these calculations:

$$2 \times 7 \times 6$$

$$3 \times 4 \times 5$$

$$9 \times 8 \times 2$$

I can multiply the numbers in any order and still get the same answer.

I will try to use times-tables that I know.

219

End of unit check

1 What is the missing number?

$$\boxed{} \times 6 = 30$$

A 24 **B** 6 **C** 4 **D** 5

2 Which number is missing from each calculation?

$$4 \times \boxed{} = 4 \qquad 5 \times \boxed{} = 5 \qquad 11 \div \boxed{} = 11$$

A 0

B 1

C 10

D A different number each time.

3 Which calculation does not work out the total number of hearts?

A 6 × 6 **B** 6 × 3 **C** 9 × 2 **D** 2 × 9

4 An athlete runs 12 kilometres (km) every day for 7 days.

How many km does the athlete run in total?

A 12 km   **B** 19 km   **C** 84 km   **D** 96 km

5 What is 4 × 3 × 5?

A 12   **B** 17   **C** 55   **D** 60

6 A box contains 72 marbles.

The marbles are shared equally between 9 bags.

How many marbles are there in each bag?

There are ☐ marbles in each bag.

7 The scales are balanced.

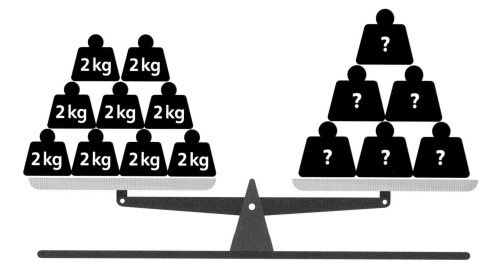

What is the mass of one of the bigger weights?

The mass of one of the bigger weights is ☐ kg.

221

→ Practice book 4A p162

It didn't matter if I made a mistake. I tried again.

What have we learnt?

Can you do all these things?

⚡ Round numbers to the nearest 10, 100 and 1,000

⚡ Compare and order numbers to 10,000

⚡ Solve addition and subtraction problems

⚡ Measure and compare the area of shapes

⚡ Multiply and divide numbers up to 12

I tried everything and learnt lots!

Now you are ready for the next books!

Published by Pearson Education Limited, 80 Strand, London, WC2R 0RL.

www.pearsonschools.co.uk

Text © Pearson Education Limited 2017, 2022
Edited by Pearson and Florence Production Ltd
First edition edited by Pearson, Little Grey Cells Publishing Services and Haremi Ltd
Designed and typeset by Pearson and Florence Production Ltd
First edition designed and typeset by Kamae Design
Original illustrations © Pearson Education Limited 2018, 2022
Illustrated by Laura Arias, John Batten, Paul Moran and Nadene Naude at Beehive Illustration;
and Florence Production Ltd and Kamae Design
Cover design by Pearson Education Ltd
Front and back cover illustrations by Diego Diaz and Nadene Naude at Beehive Illustration.
Series editor: Tony Staneff; Lead author: Josh Lury
Authors (first edition): Tony Staneff, Josh Lury, Neil Jarrett, Stephen Monaghan, Beth Smith
and Paul Wrangles
Consultants (first edition): Professor Liu Jian and Professor Zhang Dan

The rights of Tony Staneff and Josh Lury to be identified as authors of this work have been
asserted by them in accordance with the Copyright, Designs and Patents Act 1988.

First published 2018
This edition first published 2022

26 25 24 23 22
10 9 8 7 6 5 4 3 2 1

British Library Cataloguing in Publication Data
A catalogue record for this book is available from the British Library

ISBN 978 1 292 419 541

Printed in the UK by Bell & Bain Ltd, Glasgow

For Power Maths online resources, go to:
www.activelearnprimary.co.uk

Note from the publisher
Pearson has robust editorial processes, including answer and fact checks, to ensure the accuracy of
the content in this publication, and every effort is made to ensure this publication is free of errors.
We are, however, only human, and occasionally errors do occur. Pearson is not liable for any
misunderstandings that arise as a result of errors in this publication, but it is our priority to ensure
that the content is accurate. If you spot an error, please do contact us at resourcescorrections@
pearson.com so we can make sure it is corrected.